Praise for China Uncovered

'An unbelievable economic performance in co... huge potential for the future has brought China to the top of the list of every major company in the world. This book gives a detailed insight into the experiences of companies in China in terms of the cultural background, management strategies, HRM policies and on how to operate. It is an excellent and complete book and a must read for everybody involved on China – government officials, academics and students as well as business people.'

> Rob Westerhof, former CEO Philips China

'This book is a must, if your company wants to do serious business in China. Jonathan Story's book uncovers many of the pitfalls when you intend to do business in China. The practical and detailed nature of the book makes it very useful even for people who thought they knew all about China. The book is impressive with its many detailed and relevant comments from business leaders who have learned their lessons the hard way. You cannot be successful in China just by sitting in your armchair in the West, because things are so different. Personal contacts and visible leadership are extremely important.'

> Jørgen M. Clausen, Chairman, The Danfoss Group

'A compact work loaded with hands-on, actionable advice taking much of the mystery out of China. Whether you are negotiating a JV, investing in a WOFE, acquiring a local competitor or starting your own venture, *China Uncovered* is a solid starting point for your China business adventure.'

> Tomas Casas Klett, entrepreneur in China and lecturer at the University of St. Gallen, Switzerland.

'Jonathan Story has been studying the fast change of China from different perspectives and for many years. His research has now produced another masterpiece that can help executives and board members to have a more complete understanding of how their decisions will interact with the Chinese business, social, political, cultural reality today.'

> Pedro Nueno
> Executive President, CEIBS. Shanghai

Joseph Morone, CEO Albany International

'Professor Story strikes a rare balance between scholarship and business. *China Uncovered* grounds detailed, practical advice on how to do business in China in rich, historical and political analysis. This is a terrific book for anyone – practioner and scholar alike – striving to reach beyond the usual cliches about doing business in China to a deeper understanding of the forces at work in contemporary China.

'Ever wondered why your people on the ground in China aren't making greater progress? Prof. Story reveals all and explains what those back at HQ should be doing.'

EDWARD RADCLIFFE
Partner
Vermilion Partners Limited

China Uncovered

Prentice Hall

FINANCIAL TIMES

In an increasingly competitive world, we believe
it's quality of thinking that gives you the edge – an
idea that opens new doors, a technique that solves
a problem, or an insight that simply makes sense
of it all. The more you know, the smarter
and faster you can go.

That's why we work with the best minds in
business and finance to bring cutting-edge
thinking and best learning practice to a
global market.

Under a range of leading imprints, including
Financial Times Prentice Hall, we create world-
class print publications and electronic products
bringing our readers knowledge, skills and
understanding, which can be applied whether
studying or at work.

To find out more about Pearson Education
publications, or tell us about the books you'd like
to find, you can visit us at
www.pearsoned.co.uk

China Uncovered

What you need to know to do business
in China

Jonathan Story

**Financial Times
Prentice Hall**
is an imprint of

Harlow, England • London • New York • Boston • San Francisco • Toronto • Sydney • Singapore • Hong Kong
Tokyo • Seoul • Taipei • New Delhi • Cape Town • Madrid • Mexico City • Amsterdam • Munich • Paris • Milan

PEARSON EDUCATION LIMITED

Edinburgh Gate
Harlow CM20 2JE
Tel: +44 (0)1279 623623
Fax: +44 (0)1279 431059
Website: www.pearsoned.co.uk

First published in Great Britain in 2010

© Jonathan Story 2010

The right of Jonathan Story to be identified as the author of this work has been
asserted by him in accordance with the Copyright, Designs and Patents Act
1988.

ISBN: 978-0-273-70827-8

British Library Cataloguing-in-Publication Data
A catalogue record for this book is available from the British Library

Library of Congress Cataloging-in-Publication Data
A catalog record for this book is available from the Library of Congress

10 9 8 7 6 5 4 3 2 1
14 13 12 11 10

Typeset in 8/11pt melior by 30
Printed and bound by Ashford Colour Press, Gosport

The publisher's policy is to use paper manufactured from sustainable forests.

Contents

Additional resources

Over the years Story Productions Ltd. has produced a number of documentaries on the theme of doing business in China. These are highly relevant for business people wanting to understand the practical day-to-day realities of doing business in China.

All of the footage we produced is now available on our companion website, along with our China blog, an interactive investment tool and much much more. We would like to thank UK Trade and Investment (UKTI) who commissioned the documentary *China: business perspectives*, for their generosity in making the film available on the internet.

You can find this resource at: www.chinauncovered.net and follow us on Twitter @chinauncovered

Foreword

How can we develop our strategy for a country as complex and multifaceted as China? Many business people ask this question. An answer requires us to look at a much broader canvas than we conventionally do when we consider business strategy. Conventional business strategy divides conveniently into three parts, like Caesar's description of Gaul: what's going on inside the corporation; what is happening in terms of competition in the firm's markets; and, by deduction, what both enquiries hold for the firm's future.

Why is this conventional approach inadequate in the case of China? Indeed, we may ask why such an approach is inadequate – to say the least – anywhere in the world? We can provide an initial answer by asking the question of business that the Prussian theoretician and student of Napoleonic war, Clausewitz, asked: what is the essence of war? 'Frictions' was his answer, all the unexpected events that make the experience of battle one of chaos unleashed. So what is the essence of business? My reply is that the essence of business activities, very different to warfare, is to have to deal with a future about which we know little, because that is where risk and reward lie. The future of the firm is going to be shaped, yes, by firm-level decisions and competition in its specific markets, but the firm's leadership will also know that its activities will be conditioned by the dynamic contexts in which it operates. As I argued in *The Frontiers of Fortune* (Pitman, 1999), business, markets and politics dance forever together. It follows that the activity of corporate strategy is to make the world as it is the stuff out of which policy is made.

So when the chief executive of a Fortune 500 company suggested that I write a straightforward book on how to go about business in China, I decided to take on the challenge. Things in China are changing day by day, so a book describing how to set up operations in China will be out of date before it has even arrived in the bookshop. Instead of yet another set of instructions to follow, you need to know how to *think* about China, and this book is designed to show you exactly that. To borrow an old saying, I'm going to teach you how to fish.

I have been watching China since the early 1980s, and have interviewed countless managers of companies large and small who have gone into the country. Some have been burned, some have been defeated, but others have found the secret of operating in China. Unfortunately for you, that secret is different for every company and every location. What is universal is an ability to learn and adapt, an ability to execute and, above all, a clear understanding of how the China operation fits into the global organisation.

Thanks

I would like to thank INSEAD Research Committee for supporting my case studies written over the past decade on China, and the work on this book. I am particularly indebted to the China European International Business School (CEIBs), based at Shanghai, and to Rolf Cremer, dean of CEIBs. CEIBs is a great platform to get to know business people from all over China. I have also been active in courses organised at the Fontainebleau campus under the aegis of the Euro-Asia Centre, and dealing with China and Asian business conditions. Nicholas Story produced a documentary for UK Trade and Industry, entitled *China: Business Perspectives*, which is based on interviews. The documentary, like this book, aims to help business people learn about what you would have to expect if you decide to set up shop in China. It is accompanied by mini-case studies, designed for interactive learning.

Many people have been kind enough to be interviewed in the course of writing this book, whom I would like to thank: Sven and his daughter, Kristina Köhler, of Klako Group, the outsourcing and consulting services company; Gerald Kaufmann, general manager of Liaoning RHI Jinding Magnesia; Jørgen M. Clausen, Chairman, The Danfoss Group; Mogens Perp Paulsen, President, Danfoss,

China; Danfoss China vice-president, Niels-Erik Olsen, and Danfoss China vice-president sales, Arthur Xu; Bill Hoover, former director, McKinsey's, Scandinavia; Wangqiu Song, president, Stora Enso, China; Humphrey Lau, China president, Novozymes; Michael Sagan, area manager Central China, Ikea China; Viswar Kumar, deputy trading area manager, Ikea China; Eric Melloul, China director of marketing, InBev; Max Gattein, president, Europe China Convergence; Enrico Perlo, president, Guala Closures, China; Mark Siezen, managing director, REDEVCO Europe; Michael Barbalas, president of the American Chamber of Commerce, China; architects Michael Kwok and Rory McGowan from the China offices of ARUP, the global architect firm; Scott Kronick, president, China Ogilvy PR; Rob Westerhof, former CEO Philips, Greater China; Patric Dougan, general manager and China business development director, Scottish & Newcastle Asia; Ms Hong Chen Jin (Margaret Chen), alternate director, Telefonica, China; Ed Radcliffe, Partner, Vermilion, Partners, the China Corporate Finance advisory firm; Jagdish Acharya, VP Berger Paints, for China, South Pacific and Australia; and Manish Mehra, CEO, Berger Paints China; Kabir Nath, president of Bristol-Myers Squibb China (BMS); Nicholas Musy, MD, Swiss China Gateway; Steve Gilman, CEO B&Q Asia Limited; Fraser White, chairman of DMI and Dulwich College Management China; Gonzalo de Arana, former MD of Felix Solis, China; Bill Thompson, CEO, InBulk Technologies, and executive director, Clyde Blowers, China; Keith Linch, chief architect, Robinson JZFZ China; Alan Hepburn, MD, Three on the Bund, Shanghai; Mark Johnson, MD, Sigma Precisions Components. I must also thank my research assistants, particularly Rafael Bueno Martinez, Bing Xie, Hans Meyerhans, Adam Pearson, of the Boston Consulting Group, Emilio Manso-Salinas, Jocelyn Probert, and Natasha Lee-Evans who have written cases with me on China over the past decade or so. Jim Ruderman, Stephan Faris, Federica Bianchi and Nicholas Story have helped on the interviews. Kate Kirk and Sally Simmons, director of Cambridge Editorial Partnership, have greatly helped in the writing of this book. I would also like to thank Simon Rodan in working with me over ten years ago on what has become the globalisation software, presented in the last chapter. I would also like to thank William Fisk and his team at INSEAD who have worked on setting up the software for open source use and making it readily accessible over the internet.

In conclusion, I would like to dedicate this book to my lovely wife Heidi, and to our growing family, Henry, Christina and Marcel, Nicholas and Isabel, Alex and Nadine, and to our grandchildren, Louis, Marius, Stella, Joshua and Amadeus.

Jonathan Story
Fontainebleau, France and Troy, New York, July 2009.

About the author

Jonathan Story holds the Marusi Chair for Global Business and International Political Economy at the Lally School of Management and Technology, the business school of Rensselaer Polytechnic Institute, and is Emeritus Professor of International Political Economy at INSEAD. Professor Story is the author of many books, chapters in books and articles. Two companion volumes of his to this book are: *China: The Race to Market* (Pearson, 2003) about the country's transformation, and *The Frontiers of Fortune* (Pitman, 1999), which is about corporate strategy and policy in the world political economy. He co-founded Storyproductions, which produces business documentaries including *China: Business Perspectives*, made for UK Trade and Investment in 2006. These documentaries are made to help managers learn about real-life business situations. He has created a software program, presented in this book, to assist company boards craft their strategies to local conditions, and works with governments, international organisations and multinational corporations. He is married with four children.

Introduction

Why China?

In the bad old days, we used to talk about less developed countries, or newly industrialised countries, or even, shame on us, Third World countries. The capitalist West, Japan and Australasia made up the First World, the communist-socialist bloc the second and the third was made up of everyone else, typically underdeveloped countries in Africa, Asia and Latin America. The fall of the Berlin Wall in 1989 and the dissolution of the Soviet Union in 1991 were perhaps the most dramatic symbols of a changing world order, but gradual change elsewhere has seen what were once considered backward, low economy countries become known as 'emerging markets'. With home markets becoming saturated, many companies are looking at emerging markets as their next opportunity for growth, both through the competitive pricing edge that sourcing products in a low-cost country can provide and as sales territories with rising per capita incomes and consumption.

China is the most dynamic of the emerging markets. Double-digit growth and market transformation have made it no longer just the place for cheap labour and raw materials, but also home to a vast population crying out for new products. China's newly entrepreneurial workers have rapidly increased disposable incomes and greater access to international media, giving them a rising awareness of foreign brands and a keenness to buy.

> China's explosive growth is accompanied by some mind-boggling numbers

China's explosive growth is accompanied by some mind-boggling numbers. In May 2007, China's foreign exchange reserves were reported as topping $1.2 trillion, with total foreign direct investment that year to the mainland and Hong Kong combined reaching $118 billion – 43 per cent of the total of foreign direct investment flowing to Asia. By the time of the August 2008 Beijing Olympics, the foreign exchange reserves were upwards of $1.8 trillion, and figures gave $143 billion for foreign direct investment flows, or 44 per cent of the inward flows to Asia. The guesstimated total cost of the Games at a record $40 billion, showed similar growth, dwarfing the official budget of around $2 billion. By the end of 2008, official foreign exchange reserves were at $2 trillion.

And it's not just the government that has money to spare, many state-owned companies also have full coffers, and have started shopping around the world. Lenovo bought IBM's personal computer division for over $1.25 billion, the Aluminium Corporation of China, Chinalco, joined with US aluminium company Alcoa to buy a 12 per cent stake in Anglo-Australian mining company Rio Tinto for $14.05 billion and the Huaneng Group acquired the Singaporean company Tuas Power for over $3 billion, beating Indian and Bahraini firms in the final bidding.

Foreign companies are expanding their presence all over China. Special economic zones have spawned networks of suppliers and manufacturers, global companies are leveraging their China operations both within China itself and around the world, and WTO accession is removing the vestiges of protectionism and bringing the Chinese corporate legal system into line with the rest of the developed world. What's not to like?

Why not China?

Emerging markets are characterised by poor infrastructure, lack of reliable market data, weak distribution systems, poor communications, a lack of regulatory discipline, a tendency for regulations to change and a high risk of counterfeiting – and China has all these. Emerging markets are by definition developing, but just because China resembles how Western countries such as the US were thirty or fifty years ago, there is no reason to assume that China's development will bring it to the same place and all these problems will be solved.

Risk is inherent in the China decision. Some risks are universal and come with any major business investment, some are typical of an emerging market, such as scarce resources or a poor welfare system, and some are unique to China, such as the potential for a Sars disease outbreak or the challenge of protecting technologies. Many commentators are wondering if these risks indicate that China's exponential growth is built on weak foundations.

China is far from homogenous. You will read later about the need to 'show one face to China', but China will never show one face to you. Geography, resources, incomes, language, culture and customs have created a heterogenous set of distinct markets, and what sells in a first-tier city such as Beijing or Shanghai may not sell in a second- or third-tier city such as Wenzhou or Dalian. While the government's 'Go West' policy is opening up the interior to foreign companies, incomes, infrastructure and logistics are hugely variable and the chances of creating a national brand across China are limited. In addition, the many layers of government are not only complex, but also differ from region to region, and what is handed down as regulation in Beijing may not be implemented inland.

Some labour is still cheap, but you have to look harder to find it, and it may not be available in the right location for your company. Wages and other human resource costs in coastal cities and special economic zones rose rapidly during the 'boom' years, until the slowdown. Opting for a location with lower labour costs may bring with it weaker infrastructure and greater distribution overheads.

Political stability is not a new experience for China, but must be viewed through the lens of history, for some periods of stability are more equal than others. The change from a planned economy to a market system is uncharted territory and appears to make political change imperative.

Some commentators believe that the regime itself is incapable of change

Some commentators believe that the regime itself is incapable of change and China will collapse when the unstoppable force of market change meets the immovable object of the communist regime. I disagree – China is full of paradoxes, the ultimate being that the Chinese Communist Party has kept the same structure and norms as before, but there is now a different type of person holding the reins of power. Senior party members are better educated, more pragmatic and have different objectives to the old guard – the object is not immovable at all, but we're not sure where it's going.

Rule of law is new to China, and the nascent legal system is under pressure to meet World Trade Organisation (WTO) accession requirements as rapidly as possible. Bringing the law, the legal profession and corporate China into line is no simple task, and the pressures for speed will cause problems when reality does not match expectations. Equally, the tax system is adjusting to WTO norms, and retrospective tax changes can be applied at will.

Another risk is competition. There is a tendency among Chinese consumers to prefer 'national champions' to multinationals. At the same time, copying is rife, and many foreign companies have seen similar products to their own appear on the shelves very quickly. Price wars are intense and seemingly illogical when Chinese state-owned companies with little incentive to earn profits enter the fray. Nor will setting up in China necessarily give you a price advantage back home because Chinese firms are now competing globally – Haier accounted for half of the US small refrigerator market in 2002, and Galanz made one in three of the microwave ovens sold worldwide in the same year.

The stuff of business

It's not easy to learn about doing business in China, so instead of issuing instructions, my aim is to give you the tools to make the best decisions under the particular circumstances you and your company will face. By the end of the book, you'll be ready to answer what is probably your first question: should I go into China? Bear with me, there's a very important reason why we're not going to answer that question first – you need to start thinking like the Chinese. That means putting the big picture first and, for China, the big picture is transformation, so that's where we'll start.

Transformation: why operating in China is 30% plan, 70% trial and error

We don't ride in anyone else's car.

Deng Xiaoping

China is different. I'm not going to begin to count the ways, but everyone who goes to China has a tale to tell. There are horror stories about stolen machinery and disappearing salespeople, there are also fairytale endings when the products are shipped on time and staff stay loyal for years. It's tempting to think that business difficulties in China are down to bad luck, but the number of Westerners I've heard complain that their Chinese counterparts don't do things 'the right way' suggests a different reason. Far too many companies go to China and make the same mistakes a thousand others have made because they're lazy and cheap. They don't bother to invest the time and resources necessary to do even the most basic due diligence on China and they end up wasting far more money in costly mistakes.

A lot has happened over the past three decades, but China is still going through a transformation that cuts across social, commercial, economic and political spheres. In a recent leap, the Central Committee finally yielded to pressure and began to reform land ownership outside cities. Farmers will have the same rights as city dwellers, creating a market in agricultural land that is expected to lead to more efficient farms and a surge in new businesses in rural areas.

What are the implications of this? How do you begin to understand what this might mean for your business? I would contend that, since the environment for business affects how it operates, and since China's transformation defines the business system, then you have to understand what lies behind this and all the other reforms that have created today's China. You need to know where China has come from because it influences where China is going. And while you should, of course, look at the economic miracle that is China, you must also explore the darker side, the less attractive implications of transition for both business and the Chinese people.

China's transformation is happening alongside a global transformation, so, in fact, the big picture is not China but the world. Let's start there.

All change: a double transformation

China and the rest of the world are adapting to new regimes, new markets and new commercial realities, and this parallel transformation is marked on both sides by four distinct, but inter-related elements.

The first element in global transformation is change to the nation state system. We have watched the communist state system collapse, the US rise to primacy, and the fragmenting of political authority as the number of states and the variety of international regulatory bodies multiplies. Second, we see a retreat to 'market democracy', as various forms of despotism collapse, populations become better informed, market scope widens and institutional competition takes its toll. Third, a world market is being re-established under the aegis of the Western powers, and the US in particular, to a level of integration unknown since the first decade of the twentieth century. The fourth element is the growth of the industrial or service corporation, from a home country organisation with subsidiaries or market outlets in host countries to a transnational group with subsidiaries and markets located around the globe, with a widely dispersed shareholder community and a non-national recruitment policy.

China's transformation is also characterised by four distinct, but related and synchronous features. First, China is moving from a socialist command economy to a market economy under the direction of the Chinese Communist Party (CCP). This entails destroying old socialist gods, making nationalism the new binding ideology carefully adapting policy to changing conditions, and fostering institutions and habits to go with the new ways of thinking. Second, China is in transition from isolation – autarky –

China is in transition from isolation – autarky – to interdependence

to interdependence, as the country is drawn into the vortex of the Asia-Pacific and global economy. Third, China is undergoing a transition from a rural to an urban society. While disbanding Mao's collective farms has meant a return to net food self-sufficiency, this has also resulted in a huge surplus rural population that must be brought into the economy as an urgent priority. The CCP scarcely needs reminding that its own revolution was predicated on fomenting and exploiting the discontent of the rural masses, and the recent announcement by the Central Committee that it will 'transform the entire rural policy' is aimed at maintaining stability. Fourth, China is moving from membership of the international communist system to full participation in a global polity.

Table 1.1 A double transformation: China and the world

	The post-Cold War state system	The democracy wave	Re-creation of the world market	Growth of transitional corporations
Exit from the command economy	No alternative	Resist	Maximise benefits of participation in	Learn from
From autarky to interdependence	Develop multi-faceted foreign policy	Postpone	Open Door policy	Choice production and export location
Transition from rural to urban society	Communist party control over process	Control widening of liberties	Maximise comparative advantage	Promote competitive market economy
Membership of global polity	Join all regional and global institutions	Firm advocate of non-intervention principle	Co-participate in setting policy	Make global companies allies

This double transformation, illustrated in Table 1.1, has not gone unnoticed by China's leaders, and they have been quick to respond to changes in the global system. For instance, the collapse of the Soviet Union accelerated China's exit from a command economy, encouraged the development of a multifaceted foreign policy, reinforced the leadership's determination to keep control of the process, and shaped China's resolve to join regional and global policy institutions. The CCP leadership continues to resist democracy, but civil liberties in China are gradually widening, leaving the democracy option open for the future. The principle of non-intervention in the internal affairs of states is a consistent refrain through both domestic and foreign policies, yet China also seeks to maximise the benefits of participation in global markets. It is busily deepening the 'Open Door' policy, making best use of China's comparative abundance of cost-effective labour, and participating in global affairs. Over time, China's policy towards global corporations has evolved from encouraging inward technology transfer to promoting China as a location of choice for foreign investment, while at the same time pushing hard to develop a highly competitive domestic market. This combined policy sharply reduces the chances that global companies will dominate China's markets, but at the same time uses them to access the global polity.

China's adaptation is a magnificent achievement, all the more so because, critically, it has been largely reactive rather than proactive. China's leaders could not have anticipated the future of their country with any certainty in a world driven by major demographic shifts, permanent technological innovation, the scramble for natural resources to feed global demand, the dynamics of global markets, the complex workings of global politics, the re-awakening of religion as a feature of world affairs and the continued din of clashing ideologies. Faced with an uncertain future, Marxist ideology could not provide the answers, and a new pragmatism, based on 'learning from facts' through Marxist-tinted spectacles, had to be adopted. In short, China's development is about trial and error, as both China and the rest of the world learn about themselves and each other.

Transition: building socialism with Chinese characteristics

Having seen how China's transformation is intertwined with that of the wider world, it is time to take a closer look at what has been happening in China itself. To many, the economic and political transformation in China that began with the death of Mao Zedong in 1976 almost defies imagination. In just over thirty years, China has gone from number thirty-two on the world exporters league table to number three (behind Germany and the US), more than 400 million people have been lifted out of poverty, growth in gross domestic product (GDP) has been fastest in the world since 1980, and, on purchasing power parity (PPP), China has overtaken Japan as the second-largest economy in the world.

This new China is a curious mixture, a seemingly schizophrenic country, that began its transition from a centrally planned economy to something that people in the West recognise as having capitalist market drivers, yet it is still a communist state. Some commentators suggest China is gradually becoming 'more like us', with goods, tastes and policy instruments converging. The world, they claim, is becoming 'common marketised' (Fukuyama, 1989) and China is no exception to the trend. As a result of the reforms introduced by the CCP itself, the private choices of citizens now lead the market on which government's strategy is predicated (Hale, 2003), shifting the balance decisively against the regime's ability to survive in its present form. China's convergence on Western-style societies' economies will inevitably lead to a recognisable 'market-democracy'. Others take the opposite view, that China will never be 'like us', its transformation is path-dependent and China will develop a unique business system of its own (Redding, 2002). The cultural and social legacies of Confucianism and Maoist communism will continue to pervade its political and economic life, so emergence of a Western-style 'market democracy' is highly unlikely. So far along the path of China's transformation, China is neither one nor the other: it is an Adam Smith economy run by a Marxist-Leninist-Maoist party-state. As Deng put it, 'We don't ride in anyone else's car.'

Looking back (see Table 1.2) there have been four periods in the transition: the first was when Deng Xiaoping outmanoeuvred Mao's anointed successor, and opened the door to partial criticism of Mao. In the 1980s, the second period, Deng sought to balance the factions in the party-state that supported or opposed Deng's gradualist market-opening policies. But inflation rates rose and corruption erupted as parallel markets developed alongside the planned economy, ending in the dramatic events of May–June 1989, when the students assembled on Beijing's Tiananmen Square and challenged the party-state to reform in the full glare of the world's media. After some prevarication, Deng ordered the army to crush the student movement by force. Following the violence, the party-state conducted widespread arrests to suppress protesters and their supporters. It also purged party members who sympathised with the protesters. The third period opened in early 1992, a few weeks after the dramatic collapse of the Soviet Union, when Deng made his last significant contribution to the transition process on his famous 'southern tour' when he was reported as stating that 'development is of overriding importance'. A year later, a renewed leadership elaborated a policy framework to transform China into a 'socialist market economy', opening China to inward direct investment. As China's integration into the world economy gathered pace, the leadership decided in 1998, in the midst of the East Asian financial crash, to negotiate the country's entry to the WTO. The fourth period opens with China's accession to the world body in 2002. Let's trace some of the changes in China's business context, using this scheme.

Table 1.2 The road to transformation

Period	Policy change
Decision to change: 1977–79	Deng takes control: The Four Modernisations slogan replaces class war
Deng balances party factions: the 1980s	More market introduced alongside the planned sector
Jiang Zemin's 'socialist market economy': the 1990s	Marketisation and rapid emergence of the private sector
China accedes to the WTO: 2002 and beyond	The party-state signs up to global norms. High growth

The decision to change: 1977–79

The launch of reform in China is largely accredited to one man. Mao's anointed successor was Hua Guofeng, but it was Deng Xiaoping who opened the door to public criticism of Mao's failed Cultural Revolution when he launched the 'Beijing Spring' in 1977. Hua Guofeng was outmanoeuvred and effectively removed from the leadership in 1980. By this time, Deng had reopened China-US relations by becoming, in 1979, the first senior CCP figure to visit the US, demonstrating that he was not just focused on internal reform. China's new position on the world stage was subsequently confirmed when Deng negotiated the return of Hong Kong and Macau to China, under the previously unimaginable 'one country-two systems' banner. Meanwhile, Deng carefully introduced reforms in the constitution and working of the party-state, pronouncing that Mao, the architect of the Chinese revolution, was 'seven parts good, three parts bad'. While remaining Marxist-Leninist-Maoist, and still reasoning to itself in Marxist terms, the party created its own version of a multi-class society and moved away from Mao's obsession with class war at home and abroad. The class struggle was replaced with the battle for economic development, expressed as the fight to 'increase the productive forces'. This emphasis on economic growth was encapsulated in the slogan of the 'Four Modernisations', in agriculture, industry, science and technology, and the military, through which China was to achieve great power status by 2020.

Deng's grip on power was such that he was able to bring a new pragmatism to decision-making. Announcing a move towards 'socialism with Chinese characteristics', Deng essentially admitted that pure communism was no longer working, and that following the communist ideal was not always the best solution. Common sense was to be permitted to win over ideology. This attitude was epitomised in his famous comment, 'I don't care if it's a white cat or a black cat. It's a good cat so long as it catches mice.'

Deng balances party-factions: reform in the 1980s

However, pushing through such reform was not easy. Having himself been, as he put it, 'toppled' from the party three times, Deng knew only too well the importance of keeping hard-liners at bay, and was a master at pronouncements that satisfied both those who subscribed to reform and those who were dead set against change.

Why do some people always insist that the market is capitalist and only planning is socialist? Actually they are both means of developing the productive forces. So long as they serve that purpose, we should make use of them. If they serve socialism they are socialist, if they serve capitalism they are capitalist.

Selected works of Deng Xiaoping, volume 3

Deng's comments on the planned economy illustrate his skill at balancing out all interests in the party-state (Shirk, 1992). This was no easy task. China's size has always meant that central government granted a considerable amount of autonomy at the lower levels of administration. So while top-down reform in the former Soviet Union stumbled, Deng's reforms succeeded because the structure inherited from Mao was much more de-centralised and because reforms started from the ground up – often independently of the central authorities. Ideological reform permitted peasants to sell their excess produce on the open market and allowed farmers to rent out their land. This aroused the market initiative of 800 million peasants, prompting a rapid rise in rural incomes and output.

Reforms in the industrial sector were less straitghtforward: until the 1980s, manufacturing at the local level, below the giant state-owned enterprise (SOE), was in the hands of commune and brigade enterprises. In the early 1980s, these were disbanded and replaced by the town and village enterprise (TVE), which was essentially a hybrid between public ownership and private entrepreneurship, with local government owning the TVE but the manager essentially operating a private company. There were 1.4 million TVEs in 1983, but as business in the countryside was liberated, the numbers rocketed to 6.4 million in 1984 and 24.5 million in 1993. By 2006, TVEs were reported to have created 146 million jobs and accounted for 28 per cent of total employment in China.

The number of people living below the poverty threshold in China fell sharply in the 1980s. But politically inspired lending by banks surged, and inflation jumped. With corruption more visible, demands for more thorough-going reforms culminated in the movement for democratisation, secretary-general Zhao Ziyang's efforts to prevent confrontation, and finally the brutal crackdown on the students demonstrating in Tiananmen Square in June 1989.

The period 1989–92 was an anxious one for China's leadership. The violent suppression of the students prompted widespread condemnation of its actions; Japan's boom turned to bust in the summer of 1989; Germany moved fast to unity, pulling up global interest rates to fund the cost of reunification; the Soviet Union disintegrated; and the so-called 'Washington consensus' paved the way for the internationalisation of the new, US way of capitalism. All of this was important to China, because it raised the central question of which of the models among capitalist states was most appropriate for countries in transition from command to market economies. Eventually, victory in the inner-party struggles over economic policy went to the group around party secretary general Jiang Zemin.

Moving to a 'socialist market economy': the 1990s

Jiang Zemin, the future president of China (1997–2003), was instrumental in drawing up the key document of the economic transition, the 'Decision on issues concerning the establishment of a socialist market economy', which was adopted at the fourteenth party congress in November 1993, according to the *Beijing Review*. This entailed enabling the market to play the 'fundamental role in resource allocation', under the active control of the state – much along the lines of the state-led capitalisms of East Asia. In the words of the World Bank, East Asian success was due to 'the positive role of government in charting a development course' (Leipziger, 1993). Such business-friendly public policies in East Asia had yielded superior rates of accumulation of physical and human capital; rapid integration into the world economy; industrial expansion via growing export market shares; and red-carpet treatment for inward direct investors. Jiang Zemin's team from his Shanghai political base were determined that China take the same path to development.

If TVE expansion was the story of the 1980s, the growth of the private sector has been the main feature of China's economy since 1992. The importance of private enterprise to the national economy was officially recognised in 1997, and the number of registered private entrepreneurs leapt from around 90,000 in 1990 to 1.76 million in 2000. Private ownership and the rule of law were incorporated into the Chinese constitution in March 1999, and reforms to protect private property and the rights of entrepreneurs were introduced by the CCP's politburo in October 2003. By that year, the OECD, the Paris-based think-tank, calculated that the private sector was responsible for as much as 57 per cent of the value added by the non-farm business sector. Private Chinese companies were earning a 15 per cent rate of return on their physical investments, and their export-market share had jumped five times over the previous five years. Overall, the private sector, including multinationals, in China accounted for three-quarters of all exports in 2003.

> If you have a capitalist mindset, China is a wonderful place to be. In some aspects, it's more capitalist than Western Europe.
>
> Niels-Erik Olsen, vice-president, Danfoss China

A year later, CLSA brokerage concluded in the *Financial Times* that the private sector accounted for 70 per cent of China's GDP, and 75 per cent of its workforce. Foreign-owned private companies accounted for a quarter of industrial output, and were prominent, notably in the telecommunications sector. Domestic private firms were in textiles, toys, shoes, steel and accounted for three-quarters of the numbers in distribution and construction. Family landowners, the OECD report calculated, accounted for 96 per cent of farm units, but family ownership was far less prevalent in commercial services and utilities, at 39 per cent and 16 per cent respectively. The private sector is minimally present in financial services, which remains a key policy tool of the party-state, except for the venture capital market which the CCP has opened wide to entrants. The private sector has grown fastest in the eastern coastal region, where it accounted for 63 per cent of value added, against 32 per cent in other regions. In other words, the speed, specialisations and location of the private sector's emergence have been conditioned by local variants of the CCP's overall development policy.

A striking feature of China's corporate landscape in the first decade of the new millennium is the reduction in the number and weight of the SOEs. When Deng launched the reform policy, they, along with the communes, accounted for nearly all output in the country. The great purge came in the years between 1997 and 2003, when Beijing launched the policy described as '*zhuada fangxiao*', to 'grasp the large, and let go the small'. The aim was to sell off loss-making enterprises, to increase SOE efficiency in the use of capital, and to create national champions capable of taking on the multinationals. The results have been astonishing: tens of millions of workers were laid off; China's 'national champions' hold most of the shares on the Shenzhen and Shanghai equity markets, and are listed in world financial market centres; and by 2007, China featured twenty-four out of the Global Fortune 500 leading enterprises; and retained earnings was the prime source of funding of the 155 SOEs that remained under direct central government tutelage. China's industrial policy was yielding considerable dividends to the party-state in its capacity as lead shareholder.

China in the WTO: 2002 onwards

It was a new leadership team, appointed by president Jiang Zemin, that took the decision in 1998 to accelerate negotiations for China's entry to the WTO. The challenge facing the new leadership team was the combination of a financial crisis brewing as corporate debts and unsold stocks piled up on state enterprise accounts, along with the slowdown in global demand caused by the East Asian financial crash. Like previous reforms, policy change came in a bundle – foreign trade and foreign policy, domestic economic reform, personnel and administrative changes, and even some political changes. The thrust of policy was to accelerate the pace of marketisation, withdraw the government further from the market, upgrade private property rights in the Chinese constitution, reform the bureaucracy, and to move decisively, despite the leadership's initial misgivings, to join the WTO. Thereby, global norms would be incorporated into Chinese legislation and practice, while central government control over recalcitrant provincial or city governments would be reinforced.

WTO accession was the highlight of Jiang Zemin's presidency, which also saw the party endorse private business. With the handover of power to president Hu Jintao and premier Wen Jiabao in March 2003, the new leadership announced its aim of 'perfecting the socialist market economy'. The socialist component of policy was described in Confucian terms as achievement of a 'harmonious society' (*hexei shihue*). This included initiatives to improve income distribution, reduce the financial burden on farmers, narrow rural-urban income gaps, and develop the social security system. WTO entry was meanwhile followed by the rapid rise of the private sector, accompanied by development of the capital markets, and of corporate and bankruptcy law. But the heart of the transformation was for the party-state to keep the growth engine of China running – an achievement recorded by the doubling of national income in the decade 1998–2008.

The dark side

Much of what you think you know about China may be myth rather than reality.

> Much of what you think you know about China may be myth rather than reality

Although the country appears to be undergoing miraculous – and beneficial – change, a closer look reveals that things are not always as rosy as they seem. Questions arise about the numbers that define the economy, the social and environmental impacts of the transition, the continuing role of the state, corruption in private and public life, and human rights. So, what lies beneath the surface of modern China?

Despite the stunning economic growth, China remains a low income country, with per capita income by purchasing power parity less than 20 per cent of that in the US and 23 per cent of that in Japan. Those who clamour after China's 1.3 billion potential consumers would do well to remember that in reality, China's domestic market is currently comparable in size to that of Italy. There are commentators who believe Chinese consumers will bail out faltering economies elsewhere in the world, but I doubt if they would expect Italy to do the same.

Indeed, there is some question as to whether China is a market economy at all. Although recognised as such by some countries, including members of the Association of Southeast Asian Nations (ASEAN), the EU and US claim that there is still too much party-state control, particularly over certain industry sectors – notably financial services – and raw materials, for China to be classed as a market economy. They also point to the apparently WTO-compliant lower tariff rates being negated by a complex import licensing system, along with other non-tariff barriers that prevent foreign businesses from operating autonomously. Under WTO entry documents, China is officially a non-market economy until 11 December, 2016.

The numbers show that the impressive volume of exports from China is set against an equally impressive volume of imports. The vast majority of exports are in fact goods manufactured or reprocessed from imported parts and components, and sold under the names of foreign companies. HSBC reported that foreign manufacturers had more than 300,000 factories in China by the end of 2006. China's private companies are seeing their exports grow fast, but – unlike India, where Indian houses account for the bulk of exports – China's export-led growth is powered by the multinationals.

Price stability is another challenge, given the enduring imbalances in an economy undergoing root-and-branch restructuring. Periods of high inflation have been punctuated by periods of price stability and even price deflation. In 1993, cheap finance to SOEs and TVEs stoked annual inflation to 23 per cent – a dangerously high level for a country with hundreds of millions of people earning $200 a year or less. Subsequent policies to stabilise prices and shake out the inherited industrial structure were designed in part to ensure the purchasing power of China's masses. This was so successful that by the turn of the millennium there were fears of a deflationary spiral. But China's export machine, driven by high consumption and easy money in the US, picked up speed. Beijing purchased dollars in exchange for yuan on the foreign exchange markets to keep the currency low, while allowing the domestic money supply to expand. This in turn helped to stimulated super-high growth, along with a rise in inflation to 8 per cent for the first half of 2008, peaking at a twelve-year high of 8.7 per cent in February that year.

As price levels edged up, Beijing ransacked its bag of tools to bring them down. Interest rates were raised seven times in the fifteen months between mid-2006 and late 2007, price controls were reintroduced, and the People's Bank of China sold bonds to banks that could not be traded and earned no interest. Despite these measures, inflation remained stubbornly high, while useless bonds created a stagnant banking system. Critics warned about inflation stoking social unrest, and hinted that the rise in prices in China would end the supply of cheap clothing, electronics and other consumer goods flooding on to world markets. In fact, productivity in manufacturing was estimated as growing at a rate of 15–20 per cent a year (de Jonquières, 2007), thereby offsetting any increases in costs of materials and labour.

China's hyper-competitiveness on world markets is another problem. Both the US and EU agreed to bring China into the WTO with a view to encouraging Beijing to accelerate market liberalisation. Opponents of China's accession argued against, and claimed to be vindicated as China piled trade surplus on trade surplus after entry, and foreign exchange reserves soared to $2 trillion by 2009. China, they claimed, was a mercantilist and acting as a wrecker of the global trade regime. In a poll conducted by the *Financial Times* between 27 March and 8 April in 2008, in five European countries (Italy, France, Germany, Spain and the UK), 35 per cent of respondents saw China as a bigger threat to global stability than any other state (Hall and Dyer). Here was a source of protectionist sentiment that Western multinationals operating in China could not afford to ignore.

The paradox is that China's mix of policies to promote export competitiveness also makes it vulnerable to cycles in the world economy. This became evident in 2007 and 2008, as easy money conditions around the world fostered bubbles in global real estate, raw materials and oil and gas. As the bubbles began to burst, banks found their liabilities growing as their assets shrank. The US administration's decision to let Lehman's, the investment bank, go bankrupt in September spooked financial markets, and credit dried up. Export-dependent nations, including China, suddenly witnessed a shrinkage of demand from Europe and the US. The takeaway for foreign investors in China is that they have to look at the China economy as an indelibly interdependent fraction – admittedly potentially very large – of the global economy.

China's exposure to the international business cycle is equally visible in its accumulation of foreign exchange. With such reserves rising at an accelerating rate of $500 billion a year, these assets give the Chinese state the means to recapitalise banks, continue preferential lending to enterprises within the party-state family, buy US Treasury bonds, bribe dictators, bail out Western banks and purchase equity in mineral operations around the world. But it is far from clear that this accumulation of reserves – the result of the high savings, chronic surplus and foreign exchange intervention – is to China's advantage. As the former division chief for China at the IMF has repeatedly stated, the enormous holdings of US Treasury bonds leaves China vulnerable to currency movements and to US interest rate policy (Bradsher, 2008). China and the US are joined at the hip.

On the domestic side, the social effects of the transition raise a number of challenges for China's leaders. Crowded cities are becoming the norm, with the proportion of Chinese living in urban areas rising from less than 13 per cent of the population in the 1950s to around 40 per cent today. With the urban population projected to rise to 60 per cent of the total by 2030, pressure on infrastructure and social provisions will only grow. To meet the challenge, the party-state has launched a massive infrastructure development programme that will continue into the 2020s.

Rising urban populations are associated with the emergence of a new class of urban poor. Attracted to cities by the chance of high salaries – the urban to rural income gap was reported at more than three to one in 2006 – many Chinese are finding that the streets are most definitely not paved with gold. The 'iron rice bowl', social support for life once provided by the state via work units and state-owned enterprises, is no longer available as state-run companies lay off more workers than the private sector can absorb. Indeed, despite a massive shakeout of jobs, many of the state-owned companies still operating remain overstaffed, unable to innovate and rarely make a profit. If their government safety nets are removed, these companies have little chance of survival and yet more workers will find themselves out in the cold.

Attempts to address the problem of social support combine a mixture of public and private sector funding, with private employers expected to pick up where the state has left off. The new rural co-operative medical care system, designed to replace the former state-funded health system, provides subsidised medical insurance, but the more expensive the medical treatment required, the less the insurance contributes towards the cost. At the same time, private sector companies are expected to offer their workers a package of medical, housing and educational support to replace that once offered by the state. Given that private employers have been by far the largest recruiters of labour over the past two decades, it is not surprising that the party-state has sought to underpin their status as essential components of China's development.

The reality in China is that the bedrock of social policy is in effect economic growth, and growth in China is fired by the competitive dynamism of its provinces, local governments and cities. That is where local governments and developers tend to over-invest in showy real-estate projects while ignoring rudimentary environmental standards for densely populated cities. Qiu Baoxing, vice-minister for construction, said in the *Financial Times* that some 230 of the 600 or so Chinese cities surveyed by the government did not have adequate waste water treatment networks. There was, he observed, a glaring divide between local construction booms representing present economic wealth and the need for a longer-term environmental planning. According to the World Bank, sixteen of the twenty most polluted cities in the world are in China, and energy-related carbon-dioxide emissions are the second highest for an individual country. Water is also becoming more of a concern, with rivers drying up in some areas and flooding problems appearing in others. Man-made environmental problems are estimated to absorb 5–12 per cent of gross national product annually in premature deaths, healthcare costs and crop damage.

While the above apparently suggests that the party-state has just stepped back and allowed the markets to rip, this is far from being the case. China's transition is a response by trial and error to the failure of the Maoist system, with the party-state doing a lot more than simply setting parameters, and letting business work things out for itself. The CCP permeates all aspects of business, from location to marketing and from human resources to distribution. The party-state owns the land, controls where people can live, regulates raw materials and influences the economic conditions that prevail in each location through targets for economic growth and productivity. Not surprisingly, this can lead to conflict of interest, for instance in the financial system, as the party-state both owns corporate assets and controls the markets in which they are traded.

Despite central planning, there is a great deal of regional variation in how laws are interpreted and implemented. With China's size necessitating a certain amount of local administrative autonomy, we find that, while the CCP dictates, it does not necessarily control. Provincial and municipal governments must meet government targets, but the devolved administration means that central government has little say over public spending at the local level. Local authorities may find it difficult to reconcile targets for foreign investment against requirements to cut public spending, and the need to maintain social stability locally is generally more pressing than the need to placate Beijing.

The devolution of authority also means that the locus of power in China is often opaque. Deng's achievements came even though he was never officially head of state or head of the government in China. Yet he was in control of the country from the late 1970s to the early 1990s, much of the time as the Chairman of the Central Military Commission. This lack of transparency as to who actually holds power is reflected at all levels in Chinese bureaucracy, and can result in teams of negotiators spending years getting nowhere, only for it to emerge that they are not talking to the decision-makers.

There is an ideological conflict between Maoist communism and 'socialism with Chinese characteristics' that presents additional problems. Companies must obey four principles: communist party rule, the socialist road, a communist ideology, and the people's dictatorship, yet somehow these must also permit companies to do business. Private property is a case in point. Mao's legacy dictates that taking property from its owners is 'a glorious act', and if businesses are not thought to own anything, intellectual property is fair game, as is machinery and even whole factories. Yet without enforceable property rights protection, including intellectual property, economic development will stall – there is no incentive to produce if you cannot reap the benefits of ownership. The New Property Law, which came into effect in October 2007, provided a legal basis for private ownership of real estate and personal belongings, but does not solve the problem. To get the law passed, compromise had to be reached with vociferous and numerous opponents, thus it remains intentionally vague on some aspects and retains the right of the state to seize land and buildings at will for the public good.

Permission to make profits, under the 'to get rich is glorious' slogan, is a double-edged sword. While the concept it embraces has given free rein to the entrepreneurial spirit in China, it can be argued that permitting the Chinese to get rich also lies behind the rampant, costly and growing problem of corruption. While Deng did not mind if the cat was black or white as long as it caught the mouse, to many observers, the main objective seems to be for the mouse to avoid being caught by the cat.

The impression is that competitors will do what they can get away with

The impression is that competitors will do what they can get away with, until they can no longer persuade officials to look the other way.

Corruption is also linked to the endemic problem of counterfeit and fake products, which cause not only intense and irrational business competition, but also, in a few highly publicised cases, a risk to public health. In 2008, baby milk allegedly tainted with melamine to distort quality control tests was responsible for the deaths of at least four babies and illness in many thousands more. But officials have little incentive to shut down companies producing fake or sub-standard goods if they are large and provide jobs and other economic benefits to the region.

Last but not least, is China's record on human rights. These are not only a problem for the government with the increased levels of international attention that WTO accession and the Beijing Olympics have brought, but also for businesses, as activist groups seek to discover the conditions under which Nike's shoes or Gap's T-shirts are made. Companies that source goods via contractors, thus remaining at arm's length from the actual manufacturers, are also feeling the backlash as practices considered unethical to Western eyes are revealed.

Uncertainty over many of these questions is compounded by the fact that official statistics in China are notoriously fickle. Government departments collect the same data in different ways and come up with contradictory numbers. Some of the numbers are so huge that accuracy almost becomes immaterial, others are highly suspect and there is no way of checking them. Trusted sources, such as the World Bank, can more easily provide trends than absolute figures. We have to ask ourselves, do we really know anything about China?

Implications for business

Anyone who tries to predict beyond five years in China is very courageous.

Fraser G. White, founder and chief executive,
Dulwich College Management International

Not surprisingly, the complex picture that is China's transformation has implications for business. The three challenges are: change and the speed at which it is happening; the fact that China presents risks not found elsewhere; and what the future holds. All three can be summarised in one word, unpredictability. As a result, some operating factors are under management control but others are not, and it is sometimes hard to tell which is which.

Change

> We went through several changes in the retail law environment in five years, from being an 'experimental' industry in 1999, through two stages of partial deregulation to being a fully deregulated industry as of 11 December 2004.
>
> Steve Gilman, chief executive, B&Q Asia

Businesses have to cope with change in all markets, so increasing competition and tightening regulations are nothing new. But in most markets, change is steady and largely predictable, and businesses can anticipate and prepare. China's rapid and radical transformation towards a market economy has created a business environment that varies widely and changes almost daily, and there is no sign that it is slowing down.

The speed and nature of change in China is driven not only by market forces, but also by the social and political forces that constantly shape and reshape the business environment. This manifests itself in a number of ways. Political shifts can mean that what was once a favoured industry, offered incentives and exclusivity clauses, becomes a cut-throat, free-for-all. New tax regimes can turn what was a sensible five-year strategy with profits at the end into a struggle for survival. Businesses can be encouraged one day and shut down the next, not a comfortable situation to be in.

> You can plan five years ahead, but you have to update your plans every year to keep up with the pace of change. And it's different in different cities, so you have to tailor your plans for every location.
>
> Mark Ladham, retail managing director, B&Q China

Compounding the speed and unpredictability of change is the fact that business conditions are not uniform across China. While there may be comprehensive corporate, social and environmental legislation on paper, interpretation and enforcement varies from city to city and from area to area. The further west you go, the less strict things appear to be, so what your company is doing in Chongqing may not be permitted in Shanghai.

Despite all this, some business change can be anticipated. The new tax regimes needed to create parity between local and foreign businesses under WTO rules are scheduled to come into force over the next few years. Government is increasing its focus on environmental, safety and labour laws, and compliance is becoming more important. Being recognised as a market economy by 2016 will continue to force more changes that businesses can plan for. But given what we know about regional variation, we still cannot predict when the new laws will be enforced universally.

> Two years ago, a customer told me he wanted to be the biggest apple juice producer in the world. Now he is.
>
> LiLi, sales director, Novozymes China

Unusual risks

If constant change isn't enough of an unusual risk, then there are plenty of other ways that doing business in China is risky, from the nature of competition to the role of *guanxi*, and from the embryonic rule of law to the all-pervasive state. And let's not forget the watchful eyes of the world, studying carefully how businesses in China treat their employees.

> You never know how the local players are going to react. They can launch products very quickly, they can be about to launch one product and then launch something else instead. They're very flexible.
>
> Wangqiu Song, president, Stora Enso, China

Competition in China is fierce, fast and illogical, as local companies seek to get gloriously rich as quickly as possible. Chinese businesses have advantages over their foreign counterparts that they have no compunction in using whenever and wherever possible. The early open era, when inward technology transfer was the driving force of economic development, was virtually a free-for-all for Chinese businesses. Those in joint venture partnerships would be certain to have appropriated all the technology they needed by the time the original partnership ended, and stories abound of 'ghost' factories, set up in some cases next to the foreign-owned factory they were copying and containing equipment that never quite reached its official destination next door.

> Spanish confectionary company Chupa Chups found its products copied soon after launch, with names, packaging and marketing that looked on cursory inspection almost identical to the original. Having launched their lollipops at a price of 1 RMB, within three years the price was down to 0.5 RMB.
>
> Rauh, general manager, Chupa Chups, China.

The remnants of state ownership make competing on price with Chinese rivals a mug's game. Whether still state-owned or supported by easy money, many Chinese companies can cut prices to gain market share without concern for the loss of profits that entails. And it's not just price to the consumer that matters, how your products are distributed can hinge on how much you can manipulate margins along the supply chain.

> It's not easy. It's like a game – you sell your beer because you give more margin to wholesaler X and more margin to retailer Y. Your competitors are trying to do the same. It changes on a weekly basis. The margins change all the time. And it's complex because you can't do it nationally, not even at the city level, you have to do it at the neighbourhood level. And no one person can make the right decisions for 20,000 small outlets, every week.
>
> Eric Melloul, China director of marketing, InBev

Another unfair advantage for your Chinese competitors could be the fact that they probably have better *guanxi* than you. *Guanxi* is the peculiarly Chinese blend of formal and informal, social and official relationship-building that many Westerners mistakenly liken to business networking. There are many definitions of *guanxi*, but they all boil down to personal relationships, and ultimately treating people with respect. Whatever you hear about banquets and lavish gifts, that is not what *guanxi* is about and 'meat and wine' friends are not trusted. Critically, you need to develop good *guanxi* with everyone who could influence your business, and since it takes considerable time to build, your Chinese competitors will almost certainly be better connected than you.

McDonald's was delighted to be given a twenty-year lease on a prime location near Tiananmen Square in Beijing's highly desirable Wangfujing shopping district. When the store opened in April 1992, with 700 seats and 29 cash registers, it was the largest McDonald's in the world. On its opening day, 40,000 customers were served.

The company was not so delighted when, two years into the lease, it was told to shut the store down. The site was going to be redeveloped into a modern shopping centre by Hong Kong businessman Li Ka-shing. McDonald's tried to fight the order in court but failed, and by 1996 the largest McDonald's in the world had been pulled down.

One of the reasons suggested for McDonald's inability to enforce what they thought was a cast-iron agreement was that Li Ka-shing had better and more powerful connections among the decision-makers.

The reason *guanxi* still matters so much in China is because the rule of law is relatively new. Without the rule of law and the formal institutions that go with it, contracts and agreements are extremely difficult to enforce. As the McDonald's example shows, you are at the mercy of the party-state and can lose your business seemingly at a whim. And while this example is relatively old in terms of China's transition, don't forget that much of the country lags behind the major cities in the east and north, so similar conditions still prevail in much of China.

To counteract this, you must have close and comprehensive contacts with the state at all levels. We will look at this in more detail in Chapter 3, but suffice it to say that private firms need *guanxi* more than state-owned firms because they do not have the same level of protection through political connections. The strengthening of institutions to meet the needs of market and WTO compliance should eventually bring the rule of law to the fore in business situations, but it will take a long time before the threat of strangers meeting in court is more effective than the offer of a good dinner to an old friend.

An uncertain future

Having seen how the state and business are inter-related in China, it is clear that future uncertainty is not just about changing circumstances for businesses but also about how China itself copes with change. Some believe that China will converge with the West, becoming 'like us', while others believe it will diverge from the path to a market economy and either revert or become something completely different. Either way, there are economic and political challenges ahead. An *Economist* leader (2008) highlighted 'a broader awareness on the part of China's leaders of the discontented grumbling of those who feel left behind in the breakneck dash for growth'.

In *China: The Race to Market*, I put forward four scenarios for the future of China. The worst case, for China at least, I term 'sudden regime death', marked by a collapse of the communist state and civil unrest as the CCP loses control of the galloping transformation and vast swathes of the population migrate to cities in search of quick riches (this is the scenario that most concerns the leadership of the CCP). A second possibility is that China never realises its potential and remains introverted and weak, while a third is a China that threatens global stability as it reclaims Taiwan and challenges the US. Most desirable perhaps is the fourth possibility, a China that becomes a market democracy, where it demonstrates accountability and the rule of law, and the voices of the people are heard.

Each of these scenarios can be supported by a particular interpretation of circumstances. We can see that China's growth has brought financial issues that threaten economic stability. We can also see social change, with the widening income gap between rich and poor creating tension, and attempts to move people out of their houses and off land to make way for infrastructure projects are meeting with increasingly vocal opposition. But we cannot predict which, if any, of these scenarios will come to pass. What is certain is that change is irreversible. China is swept up in its own transformation, and the market and the economy cannot stand still.

Perhaps the biggest unknown is who will be responsible for the next big leap

Perhaps the biggest unknown is who will be responsible for the next big leap. Deng's path to power was anything but straight and some of his reforms could not have been imagined just a few years before he put them into action. While China's next leaders are already chosen, with analysts expecting new politburo members Xi Jinping and Li Keqiang to take the top positions at the next party congress in 2012, a BBC article (Bristow, 2007) pointed out that 'China is not good at making sure anointed leaders actually make it to the top of the political pile – several have died before being promoted.' As the article continued, '[t]here is no rule, regulation or precedent that cannot be broken or overturned – and no heir apparent that cannot fall foul of a changing political wind or another, stronger candidate.' And whoever is appointed to the top position may be irrelevant, power could stay in other, less visible hands.

China takeaways

▌ You have to learn how to think about China, and this takes time.

▌ Be prepared to explore the big picture before you get down to details.

▌ Remember that the big picture encompasses global transformation, not just China itself.

▌ Understand that there is more to come – China's political and economic transformation is still in its early stages, and the business environment can and will change many times before 'normalcy' is reached.

▌ Realise that your strategy must reflect the pace of change, the unusual risks of operating in China and an uncertain future – you won't be able to duplicate what you have done elsewhere, because China is different.

China-watching is the only profession that makes meteorology look accurate.

Nicholas Kristof, former Beijing bureau chief, *New York Times*
(Weldon and Vanhonacker)

There is one more big picture you must look at before we start getting into details – your organisation. If the only certainty is uncertainty, what type of organisation can survive in China? What capabilities do you need to negotiate the labyrinth of *guanxi*, regional differences, legal vagueness and downright surprise that is the China business environment? In the next chapter, we'll take a look at the essential requirements for a business heading into the Middle Kingdom.

References and bibliography

Bradsher, K. (2008) 'Main bank of China is in need of capital,' *New York Times*, 5 September.

Bristow, M. (2007) 'China's new faces set stage for 2012,' BBC News, 22 October.

de Jonquières, G. (2007) 'China's exporters are striking it rich', FT.com, 7 March.

Deng, X. (1994) *Selected Works of Deng Xiaoping*, Volume 3, 1982–92, Foreign Language Press, Beijing.

The Economist (2008), 'Megaphone apology – Snowbound China,' 9 February.

Fukuyama, F. (1989) 'The end of history,' *National Interest*, summer.

Hale, D., and Hale L.H. (2003) 'China takes off,' *Foreign Affairs*, Nov–Dec.

Beijing Review, 22–28 November 1993, pp.12–31

Leipziger, D.M., and Vinod T. (1993) *The Lessons of East Asia: An Overview of Country Experience*, World Bank, Washington, DC.

Redding, G. (2002) 'The capitalist business system of China and its rationale,' *Asia Pacific Journal of Management*, pp.221–249.

Shirk, S. (1992) 'The Chinese political system and the political strategy of economic reform,' in Lieberthal, K., Lampton, D. (eds) *Bureaucracy, Politics and Decision-Making in Post-Mao China*, University of California Press, Berkeley, CA, pp.77.

Story, J. (2003) *China: The Race to Market*, FT Prentice Hall, London.

Weldon, E. and Vanhonacker, W. (1999) 'Operating a foreign-invested enterprise in China: challenges for managers and management researchers,' *Journal of World Business*, 34(1), 94–107, from Garten, J. E. (1998) 'Opening the doors for business in China,' *Harvard Business Review*, (May–June) pp.167–75.

The organisation: a work in progress

> Do not repeat the tactics that have gained you one victory, but let your methods be regulated by the infinite variety of circumstances.
>
> Sun Tzu, *The Art of War*

As we've seen in the previous chapter, China is certainly full of an 'infinite variety of circumstances'. The political and economic transformation is just part of the picture for business, there are plenty of other challenges that will emerge as you go through this book. Under these circumstances, it's worth pointing out that getting the strategy 'right' in China is not the end result – what actually helps you win in China is execution. Strategy can be changed with just a few meetings and a keyboard, what takes more effort is shifting organisational capabilities to implement the new strategy, turning the proverbial tanker around. Here, we're going to look at some of the latest thinking on strategy in a changing world, and the organisational factors that will help you meet the challenges that China presents.

The China context: implications for strategy

We discussed in Chapter 1 how China's transformation creates a unique environment for business. The nature and pace of change, unusual risks and the uncertain future in China all have profound implications for corporate strategy, and you may have to change the way you think about your organisation.

To begin to develop a strategy for China, we have to take a holistic approach to strategy and policy. Traditional thinking on strategy, for instance that championed by Michael Porter (1980), is rooted in classical economics and industrial organisation and fails to take account of either time or history – two elements that are critical in China. Traditional thinking also assumes a full knowledge of market conditions, that all companies are driven by profit, and that competition in the market conditions the firm's conduct and performance, with 'government' featuring as a spanner in the works of an ideal market-clearing mechanism. Again, these don't match the reality in China – the lack of reliable data means that market conditions cannot be completely known, state-owned enterprises supported by soft money have little or no incentive to make a profit, competition may be irrational and illogical, and 'government' is not merely a spanner but all-pervasive.

Standard thinking leads to three categories of corporate strategy – cost leadership, product differentiation through superior design, quality or functionality, and focusing on one or more specific niches. Clearly, the concept of cost leadership has a bearing on China, given the territory's reputation as a source of cheap labour, but the privileged access to cheap finance available to companies within the communist party's extensive sphere of influence makes it hard for foreign companies to play this game. Superior products should be able to command superior prices, but differentiation and the accompanying price premiums are difficult to maintain as the competition moves swiftly to introduce similar products. The price premium for Japanese televisions sold in China fell from 20 per cent in 1999 to 5 per cent by 2004. With prices being eroded as local competitors advance, niche markets may not remain niche for very long. Nor do more mainstream markets in China behave as expected – in 1995, *The Economist* predicted that foreign multinational corporations would have captured 80 per cent of the Chinese personal computer market by the 2000; in reality, by 2004 they had just 20 per cent market share.

In China, any discussion of corporate strategy must take account of history, politics, institutions, culture, and, critically, what Donald Sull (2005) has referred to as the 'fog of the future'. People doing business in China must learn how to deal with a future about which little is known, but about which some things can be learnt. That can be said about doing business in many countries, what is peculiar to China is the question of which lessons from history can or should be applied to the ever-moving present. As US baseball player Yogi Berra used to put it: 'The future ain't what it used to be.'

So, we need another way of looking at the strategy question in China

So, we need another way of looking at the strategy question in China. Yves Doz and C.K. Prahalad (1987) link corporate strategy to history and past policies, structures and performances when they speak of strategy as 'the dominant world view' among senior managers. This world view encompasses the nature of competition, the success factors in sustaining a competitive advantage, the type of risk incurred, and the resource base on which managers draw. As Doz and Prahalad put it, managers must be able to 'recognise the balance of the forces of global integration and local responsiveness to which a business is subject' (1987: 30).

Chris Bartlett and Sumantra Ghoshal have gone a step further and rooted the international strategy of companies in the specifics of their home markets. During the twentieth century, European companies, such as Philips, Unilever and Nestlé, learnt to operate as de-centralised federations of subsidiaries to fit the fragmented national markets of Europe and became highly sensitive to local conditions. Such a structure proved vulnerable to cost pressures when markets opened up in the 1980s and competition sharpened. Meanwhile, US companies such as GM, Ford, IBM, Coca-Cola, Caterpillar and Procter & Gamble operated abroad as 'co-ordinated federalists', their key assets being the size of their home market, their home-based research and development, and their skill in transferring technologies to overseas markets. Headquarters controlled the main resources, and left operations to the locals, while glass ceilings kept those local managers out of senior positions.

In the 1970s, both European and US companies faced an onslaught of competition from Japanese exporters. The strategic intent of corporations such as Toyota, NEC and Matsushita was to achieve global dominance in their respective markets in order to fund a switch from competition on the basis of low labour costs towards high-technology, lean manufacturing systems. Such companies treated the world as one market. Knowledge was developed and retained centrally. Their plants were built to produce mass standardised products, which were sold using aggressive pricing strategies. Integration between the central product division and each subsidiary was achieved through top-down strategic plans and controls, the fostering of a strong corporate identity, and through socialisation of personnel. Subsidiaries were concentrated in a few locations. But such 'global strategists', as Bartlett and Ghoshal termed them, were vulnerable to trade retaliation, consumer reactions to standardised products, and to yet more glass ceilings that kept locals in very low positions in the organisation.

So what's the answer? Bartlett and Ghoshal (1989) argue for the transnational corporation, one that incorporates the best features of the European de-centralised federations, the US co-ordinated federalists and the Japanese global strategists. Thus they foster local responsiveness, knowledge management and efficiency. The transnational corporation's key feature is that it functions as an integrated network. Local units provide skills, ideas and capabilities, and attain global scale when one of their products is sold worldwide. The company adopts flexible manufacturing techniques, and takes optimum choices with regard to sourcing of inputs, pricing and product design. This implies a very different role for headquarters, as all the separate units must somehow be integrated and co-ordinated while maintaining a degree of autonomy. Transnational corporations speak English as a common language, develop inclusive management networks, acquire a corporate-wide global scanning capability, and promote a common culture through incentives, corporate visions and leadership selection. In short, they become a learning organisation in a permanent process of renewal.

This way of looking at the global organisation allows us to accommodate the contention that operating in China is 30 per cent plan, 70 per cent trial and error, and agrees with Sull's suggestion that global organisations can be paralysed by strident long-term visions – in China an obvious parallel is how Mao's Great Leap Forward and Cultural Revolution continued in the face of mounting negative feedback. So in the same way that fuzzy logic helps us when data is approximate rather than precise, Sull recommends a 'fuzzy vision', such as 'we aspire to be global leader in our industry', to provide a dominant world view that can then shape operations and processes, wherever and whatever they are. The UK's easyGroup is an example of this.

Fuzzy and easy

UK-based easyGroup includes among its brand values 'taking on the big boys' and 'keeping it simple'. The company's vision is to 'paint the world orange!' It's hard to get much fuzzier than that.

If painting the world a different colour is too scary to contemplate, then reflect on what was said earlier about China's transformation – strategy has to be formed in a changing China and in a changing world. Eric Melloul of InBev refers to his company's China strategy as an 'evolving concept', saying that it has to change – or evolve – every six months to a year. Yves Doz and Mikko Kosonen (2008) talk about 'fast strategy', or 'strategic agility', as the factor that will underlie the successful organisations of the future. They argue that striving for innovation and continuously developing capabilities are the only ways to keep ahead, and that organisations must 'perceive early, decide quickly and strike with strength and speed'. This requires senior managers who can monitor and analyse the external environment, can make commitments without being delayed by internal politics, and can mobilise the resources to back up those decisions.

Whether you go for fuzzy or fast and evolving, you and your organisation will be thrown into a constant and iterative process of learning and adapting to the whirlwind that is China.

> Your organisation will be thrown into adapting
> to the whirlwind that is China

The learning organisation

We've all heard of the learning organisation, and we probably all think we know what one is, but I doubt we would agree on the definition. In the interests of our big picture view, not only of China but also of our organisation, let's take a brief detour via some work of a former colleague at INSEAD, Edith Penrose, to show you why learning, particularly at the top of the organisation, is so important.

Penrose (1995) defined firms as bundles of resources, under managerial direction, for use of goods and services, sold in markets for a profit. Each firm is unique in the combination of resources it develops to serve the market. This is an important insight for us because it follows that the managerial resources required for the firm to expand are specific, and cannot be readily acquired.

Knowledge is built up over time through the firm's collective learning process, as projects are completed and new horizons and opportunities open up in the light of the knowledge acquired. Knowledge can be transmittable, for instance in manuals or standardised procedures, but firm-specific knowledge, based on experience in a particular organisation, with its own peculiar markets, culture and capabilities, is harder to transmit.

Firms tend to expand by diversifying into new areas of activity, which requires learning. The limits to growth are determined by the rate at which managers can plan and implement the new activities. They can of, course, hire more managers, but then they must devote time to training the newcomers in the many specific features of the firm, which takes staff away from other tasks. And it takes more time for the newcomers to learn everything they need to know. Growth is thus limited by time – the scarce resource of managers – rather than the learning process itself.

Managers select activities for expansion based on their own accumulated knowledge of the firm itself and their interpretation of the external environment as it applies to the firm. This external environment is not a 'fact', it is not known, easily analysed or accurately anticipated; it is, as Penrose suggests, an 'image' in the minds of the managers, who are looking to exploit all the productive possibilities they can see. This dynamic interaction between the internal context of the firm and an interpreted environment creates opportunities for diversification, limited only by the existing resources of the firm – confirming what Adam Smith wrote back in 1776 in Chapter 3 of *An Inquiry into the Nature and Causes of the Wealth of Nations*, that 'the division of labour is limited by the extent of the market'.

Once a firm decides to move outside its national boundaries, the same factors drive growth, but other obstacles must be faced. The role of learning, the availability of resources, the need for authoritative co-ordination of activities and the dynamic interaction between the firm's resources and the opportunities perceived by management in the environment, all these remain as before. What changes is the existence of international borders, and the need for more learning, this time about different cultures, languages, institutions and customs. Acquiring firm knowledge about these again takes time, and involves a process of trial and error, of learning by listening to the stories of other firms and managers, and of diffusing that knowledge through the firm. This is all the more relevant for firms entering a country such as China, which is undergoing its own massive learning process while shedding a failed party-state system to adopt what the regime has described as a 'socialist market economy'.

So the learning organisation is a patient organisation, taking the time and spending the money to put knowledge at the heart of all its decisions. When thinking about China, therefore, the initial focus must be on the top team's learning.

The view from HQ

I think overall there's a general understanding about the importance of China. But there's a poor understanding of what it takes to win in China. I spend a lot of my time educating people in HQ. It's difficult because they might be overseeing twenty countries, and two trips to China a year are not enough to allow them to form a decent opinion about what needs to be done.

Eric Melloul, China director of marketing, InBev

If the top team doesn't learn about China, then those lower down the ladder who are sent to get China operations up and running will be fighting a losing battle. They won't have the decision-making power, the support or the understanding to succeed. Time to look at what the top team needs to know.

I'm going to give you what appears at first to be contradictory advice – you must integrate operations globally, but at the same time, you must give your China operations enough autonomy to make decisions quickly and independently in response to whatever China throws at them. This is, in fact, Bartlett and Ghoshal's transnational corporation writ large, an integrated network of financially interdependent operations that share knowledge, innovation and success.

Integration

China operations must be integrated into global operations or they will not survive. Few China ventures undertaken by foreign companies provide the lion's share of worldwide revenues, and you should certainly not expect instant results. Sales in China usually take considerable time and investment to reach profitability, and some companies are maintaining a break-even or even loss-making operation in China because they want to be in place as the market develops.

> It is important to avoid the temptation of throwing everything at China at the expense of other regions

With this in mind, it is important to avoid the temptation of throwing everything at China at the expense of other regions, for while China is probably the main battleground in the struggle for future global market share, at this stage in China's development many companies find that other territories are more profitable. It is how China is integrated into overall sales strategies, therefore, that is critical, and you cannot do this without integrating across the organisation as a whole, including R&D, supply chain, knowledge transfer and distribution.

If the China operation is to be fully integrated, then how it reports upwards will be an important reflection of how China fits into the organisation as a whole. Some companies view China as part of the Asia-Pacific region (Asia-Pac) and the China chief executive reports to Asia-Pac rather than directly to HQ. Other companies take the view that China is a region in itself, with all its different markets and massive geography, so China reports directly to the central organisation. For instance, Asia-Pac is an important region for Bristol Myers Squibb and consequently has a strong voice at headquarters, so its operations in China report to Asia-Pac. Novozymes, on the other hand, has its China group report directly to HQ in Denmark. The position of China in the organisation does not go unnoticed by your Chinese hosts, and the stronger the connection to HQ the more the company in China will be respected. The head of Samsung in China is one of the three top decision-makers for the entire company.

Showing one face to China

At the heart of the integration-autonomy conundrum is the need to show 'one face to China'. As Ken Lieberthal, the renowned American China expert, has noted:

> Most global corporations currently downplay country management, putting more power in the hands of business unit and product line managers. China begs to be the exception to this practice, at least for now. Business unit autonomy does not work well there, because the Chinese government views corporations as single entities and largely treats them as such. Instead, it pays to show 'one face to China', that

is, to establish a corporate identity that highlights the compatibility between the company's goals and the country's goals.

While other countries can have regional and country managers, your China operation should have a senior person with a prestigious title in the organisation – who reports directly to the Chief Executive.
This direct line is vital for the China country chief to deal with the corporate global product and regional managers from a position of authority. A correct title, such as 'President' is essential for opening doors in China, conferring a status on its owner that reflects not only their own importance, but also the importance of the people they meet.

Integrating will also involve managing perceptions and expectations on all sides, not only between HQ and China, but also between subsidiaries around the world. Product managers in Brazil, for instance, may think sourcing from China will be cheap because of low unit labour costs, but from an organisational perspective it is total operating costs that count, and without this understanding, 'cheap' sourcing can become expensive.

China can appear to be out of line with corporate policy for compliance with national and international regulations, but the wider organisation must understand that in China national laws don't necessarily translate into locally enforced rules. China may also appear to have a much higher budget for human resources, recruitment and retention, and corporate entertaining, but again the Chinese realities have to be clearly understood.

Profit is growing but in absolute terms it's still relatively small. We may have 10–15 per cent of global sales volume here, but China is a high-volume, low-margin business by world standards. We're confident that margins will improve – we've invested close to a billion euros in this market, so you can see we're committed to China.

Eric Melloul, China director of marketing, InBev

One of the issues in managing perceptions and expectations for many companies is that success in China cannot be measured in the same way that it is elsewhere, and if this is not understood it can sour relationships between units. You must avoid the conflict that can arise when what HQ expects, based on experiences in other parts of the world, cannot be delivered by those on the ground in China. The reality of China must be acknowledged when corporate goals are set.

> The margin model is inverted in China: the vendor makes the most, the middleman makes the second most, and the retailer makes the least.
>
> . . . we've invested more in prices and given more to the consumer every year than we've ever taken to the bottom line. We've done that every year since we opened, and we will continue to do so. Our margins now are approaching half what the European margins are. We've practically doubled them from the early days. Our plan has always been to improve margins by about 1 per cent a year, net margin, and we've always been there or thereabouts.
>
> Steve Gilman, chief executive B&Q Asia,
> in 'Shaping China's home-improvement market: an interview
> with B&Q's CEO for Asia', *McKinsey Quarterly*, June 2006

For some companies, market share may be a better measure of success than growth rate in China. As margins start to improve, market share will be the key to distinguishing between the success stories and the also-rans, and can also prevent companies from misinterpreting their performance. Consider, for instance, the case of Danfoss, the Danish industrial controls company (Hoover, 2006). Chief executive Jorgen Clausen read an article in a newspaper about a large European manufacturer that was happy with its 40 per cent growth in China until it discovered that the entire market for its product category was growing at 80 per cent. So Clausen initiated an exploratory review of the market for Danfoss products in China and found that, despite high sales growth: 'We were just skimming the surface and capturing only a few percentage points' share in most of our product markets.'

Another reason for promoting integration across the organisation is China's critical position in the global market of the future. Given its potential significance, we can envisage a market where China leads and the rest of the world follows. In this case, lessons learnt from the experiences of operating in China could well become applicable elsewhere. A truly integrated and responsive organisation will be able to adapt the skills it has had to learn to survive in China, in particular flexibility and rapid response to change, and apply them worldwide. An organisation that takes this learning approach will integrate China better into overall operations because it will see that the traffic in management expertise and skill is not just one way.

Autonomy and control

Luckily I have a very good board in the UK, and they generally let us get on with things in China. We give a detailed report once a month on financials, marketing, staff, workload and prospects, but generally speaking the decision-making for China is left to me. **Our board and shareholders in the UK realise that the market situation is so different in China, if you're not actually working here you cannot fully understand it**. They accept that they do not fully understand everything that goes on in China, but as long as the figures look good and everything seems to be working, they are happy to let us carry on.

Keith Linch, managing director of the Chinese joint venture for UK civil engineering group Robinson

The 'imperial' model, with worldwide HQ handing down diktats and procedures, can hamper China operations, where the key to success can often be speed of response. Such a formal structure, where HQ assumes the world is one market (as it ultimately is) and operates according to one logic (which it does not), may be 'a powerful but blunt weapon for effecting strategic change'. But processes that work perfectly well elsewhere will have to be adapted, because what may be best practice in Germany or the US might not work so well in China. Products, branding and design will all need to be developed 'on the ground' rather than in an HQ building on the other side of the world. Logo, name and pricing cannot be decided in a meeting room thousands of miles away, possibly by people who have never been to China.

One of the problems this causes is evident in the names some companies have chosen for their China operations. While some have been successful in choosing Chinese words that either sound like their foreign name or mean something similar, others have been lumbered with unlucky or simply inappropriate names. Telecoms group Lucent in China is known as Lang Xun, which translates as 'bright communications', and mobile phone maker Ericsson is Ai li Xin, 'to love, establish and have confidence'. Microsoft, on the other hand, has a history of getting things wrong in China, and one of the US software group's first mistakes was to select a literal translation of its name.

> ## One of the US software group's first mistakes was to select a literal translation of its name

While *Business Week* described the company's Chinese name, Weiruan, as meaning 'little' and 'soft', hardly inspiring from one of the largest companies in the world, Rachel DeWoskin, in her book named after the Chinese soap opera she starred in, *Foreign Babes in Beijing*, points out that it could also be read as 'little and flaccid', an even less salubrious moniker. Spanish confectionary company Chupa Chups did not translate the company name on their lollipops into Chinese characters, and took several years to realise that its customers could not read or pronounce the name of the product. Customers who only recognised the stylised daisy logo could not distinguish between the real product and almost identically labelled counterfeits.

Freedom to name is one thing, but freedom to respond to circumstances is equally critical in a fast-changing environment. Reporting to Denmark and having to follow procedures and policies developed at HQ makes biotechnology group Novozymes less flexible in China and unable to react as quickly as it would like, whereas DIY retailer B&Q sees its independence in China as a competitive advantage over US competitors that not only have to refer decisions to HQ, but also have to suffer the consequences of a twelve-hour time difference as well.

> The last couple of months have been total chaos in the ports – everybody is rushing to get their goods out so they can get their VAT rebates before the rules change.
>
> Michael Sagan, Ikea area manager, Central China

Operations in China need autonomy so they can keep up with not only the pace of change, but also the pace of business. Things that might take ten years elsewhere can happen in one or two years in China.

> The turnover of projects here is much faster than back in the UK. All our clients want things quickly. In the UK, we would look at a planning process of a year. Here, that gets cut down to a matter of weeks. Some projects can go from sketch to pouring concrete on site in twelve weeks, which is unheard of in the UK. That has been a big battle for the expat staff, learning to deal with projects in a much faster timeframe and turning the work round fast enough.
>
> Keith Linch, managing director, Robinson JZFZ

Markets, too, can change very quickly. When B&Q opened in China, people bought concrete shells that they then turned into a home. But now the second-hand housing market in China is taking off – in 2003, it was almost non-existent in Shanghai, three years later it comprised 15–18 per cent of housing transactions – and B&Q has a much bigger market for kitchens and bathrooms, as Chinese homebuyers renovate the houses they have bought.

To make it more complicated, not only do markets change within themselves, but, as we described in Chapter 1, there is a considerable amount of administrative variation across China and this is reflected in regional variations in markets. As a result, B&Q views China as four regions, not necessarily a fragmented market, but one in which they need to be flexible, and thus they offer more local brands in tier-three cities than in tier-two or tier-one cities, but they expect this to change over the next five to ten years as their customers' incomes and desires change.

This suggests that product development is another area where HQ must let the China operation lead the way. US company Whirlpool's experience bears this out.

Hard lessons for Whirlpool

'We had every reason to believe we could be a top player in China. The revenue streams just didn't come as expected.' That was Whirlpool Asia president Robert Hall, commenting on a £350 million charge against earnings in 1998, about a third of which was attributed to losses in Asia, mostly China.

- **Too much too soon:** rather than launch one product and use that to learn about the Chinese market and build distribution channels, Whirlpool decided to launch four products over the space of about ten months in the mid-1990s: air-conditioning units, microwave ovens, refrigerators and washing machines.

- **Over-engineering:** instead of adjusting manufacturing to match local norms and using local resources, the company used aeronautical steel in its washing machines, high-quality aluminium foil in its air conditioners and imported chemical products from Dupont and GE, making Whirlpool appliances 20 per cent more expensive than local products.

- **Size isn't everything:** Chinese homes are cramped and the Chinese shop regularly because they prefer fresh food, so the giant 200–300 litre refrigerators offered by Whirlpool didn't fit into their lives or their lifestyles.

- **Failing to adapt:** Chinese competitors were quick to respond when they noticed unusual market conditions, such as the farmers in Sichuan province who used their washing machines to wash sweet potatoes as well as clothes. Haier adjusted the filters in their machines to cope with high levels of silt and mud, Whirlpool did not.

- **Government intervention:** Chinese competitors were given a boost by the government's exhortation to 'buy Chinese', making Whirlpool's prices even less attractive.

Another mistake Whirlpool made was not to offer the latest technology – its competitors went straight to producing and selling CFC-free refrigerators, and by the time Whirlpool had lumbered through its procedures for new product design, starting with hiring researchers, it was years behind. The vast size of the middle- and low-end markets still tempts companies who have not done their due diligence to offer old products and old technology in China. But it is far too late for such a strategy to work. The Chinese government and domestic competition have destroyed any market for old Western goods that might have existed in the early days of the new China. Now, the Chinese want the latest and most advanced products.

Now, the Chinese want the latest and most advanced products

As can be seen from the Whirlpool example, organisations have to find a way to offer their products at the kind of price that the Chinese will pay, and must think strategically about how they are going to do this. Except in a few sectors such as aerospace or medical equipment, it is no good importing raw materials, or asking European engineers to 'dumb down' a product so that it will be cheaper to make in China and therefore reach the right price point. Instead, you must offer 'born and bred' Chinese products, designed and made in China for the Chinese. Only in this way will you be able to reach those all-important, enormous markets.

Autonomy does not mean complete freedom. If exporting from China is one of your objectives, then production will have to meet global standards for quality and efficiency, and your China operation will have to recognise this and act accordingly. Best practice must be adapted for China, and systems should be integrated globally wherever possible. It is imperative to avoid getting sucked into 'China practice', where poor quality and high levels of waste and inefficiency are masked by ultra-low costs. This may be cheaper in the short term but will undoubtedly cost the organisation more in the long term, through lost customers and damaged reputation. The recalls of sub-standard and even dangerous products in 2007 and 2008 showed yet again how quickly attitudes towards 'made in China' can change, and the vigilance of activist groups that focus on working conditions and environmental compliance shows no signs of abating. Your China venture will not operate in isolation from the rest of the world, and nor can you.

If you intend to be the best restaurant in Shanghai...that restaurant better be good enough for London or New York.

Alan Hepburn, Three on the Bund, Shanghai

Visits from on high

An important part of showing one face to China is in the way visits from the chief executive, senior managers and directors are conducted. Their visits not only demonstrate the value of China operations to the organisation as a whole, but also provide opportunities to meet with senior Chinese officials, a crucial part of doing business in China that we will discuss in more depth in the next chapter. Another of Microsoft's early mistakes was Bill Gates's 1994 visit to President Jiang Zemin. While the story that he committed the ultimate insult of wearing jeans to meet the president is not true, after the visit it was announced that the president had recommended that Gates learn more about Chinese culture, a pointed comment that highlighted where Microsoft was going so wrong in its first forays into China.

Chinese staff need to feel that they are working for someone with status, so even if many of the managers in China are expats and might be satisfied with regular telephone, email and video contact, only a visit will do for local employees. Danfoss knows this well, and its website includes numerous press releases detailing visits by president and chief executive Jorgen M. Clausen, and dignitaries such as the Danish vice-prime minister, the Danish minister of the environment and the prince and princess of Denmark. These visits demonstrate not only the important role of Danfoss's China operations in the company as a whole, but also their importance to Denmark itself, putting the Danfoss-China relationship on a much higher level.

China: the 'second home market'

Danfoss intends to make China its 'second home market'. To reflect this level of strategic importance, the company has a 'Business Board' for China made up of high-level representatives from HQ, including the chief executive, chief operating officer, vice-chief executive, and three divisional presidents. Visits by the members, and in some cases their past experience working in or with China, improve their knowledge and understanding of the country and facilitate communication between HQ and China. While it is not part of the official organisational structure, the business board demonstrates the importance of China to the organisation.

If your China operation is important to you, it is not a question of visiting for a few days when you feel like it. Scheduled, structured visits, and perhaps rotating board meetings through China, will help to keep operations integrated with the rest of the organisation.

Visits can also help to open the eyes of senior management to the opportunities of China:

> The board sensed the promise of China as soon as they went out on to the streets in Shanghai. Their immediate reaction was, if that is what the wealthiest part of China has achieved, it would only be a matter of time until the rest of China catches up.
>
> Mark Siezen, managing director, Redevco Europe,
> part of Dutch retailer C&A

But there is a downside to visits. While HQ may see them as useful and productive, the China operation may see them as a cheap show organised simply to tick a box. If managers in China do not feel that they have been listened to, they will view the visit in a negative way. After all, it is hard for senior managers to understand operational constraints on a short visit where they spend half the time wining and dining local dignitaries. HQ will have to demonstrate the outcomes of the visit through strategies, policies and other operational activities that can clearly be ascribed to what they have learnt in China.

Company culture

The success or otherwise of visits will depend to a certain extent on how they contribute towards instilling corporate culture. While some companies have a strong culture of their own that they will expect China operations to absorb and emulate, others let the Chinese experience help them to build a new culture.

For organisations melding two, or possibly more, cultures in their China operations, it can be easier if the culture of the home country is radically different from that of China, because cultural differences will be expected and, at least in part, understood.

It can be easier if the culture of the home country is radically different from that of China

For countries that are culturally similar to China, such as Taiwan or Singapore, it can be harder to accept differences as simply that, differences, rather than something more threatening.

> We have our cultural problems. It has been a learning process both for us and for them and mostly, where there is a conflict due to culture, we meet in the middle. Our Chinese staff respect our cultural differences and we respect theirs, and we find a way to work together.
>
> Keith Linch, managing director, Robinson JZFZ

Company culture provides the framework for, and is defined by, intra-organisational communication. From the unwritten 'we don't do it that way' to manuals detailing procedures to the nth degree, and from a brief congratulatory memo from the line manager to a full-blown photo-opportunity with the chief, how an organisation communicates reflects how it operates. For the China operation, that communication will begin with cross-cultural training.

It is well known that cross-cultural training can be an important factor in the success or otherwise of overseas assignments. But cross-cultural training is not just for expats being posted to China, and it isn't just about language, habits and how to behave at business meetings. Cross-cultural training must also relate to corporate strategy and organisational culture both in China and in the home country, and should be provided to senior management staying in the home country as well as those going to China. This will help those in HQ to understand the challenges that their expat staff may be facing and also improve communication with Chinese staff, partners and government. And don't forget the opposite direction – the need to localise means that many companies are bringing their more senior Chinese staff to other sites around the world as part of their career development programme. These staff need cross-cultural training just as much as those going to or working with China.

Integrating employees

InBev has a 'global talent pool' programme, in collaboration with INSEAD and Wharton business schools, which acts not only as a retention tool, but also as a method of acculturating and globalising its Chinese employees. Interacting with InBev employees from around the globe helps to create a stronger corporate network, one that includes China as a functional part of the whole rather than an outpost that nobody quite understands.

It is important to keep a balanced view in all this. It's about what will work for your organisation, which you can only determine through internal consultation and external research. It is not about treating China as another planet, where normal business rules do not apply.

Do not go off and change your whole business strategy for China. Consider China nuances, but don't change the whole model to succeed in China.

Scott Kronick, president, Ogilvy PR China

Growing with China

Let's put everything together and look at a stylised view of how a company might enter and grow in China, eventually consolidating China activities into worldwide operations. This scenario is based on a company I have followed for a long time, and reflects how it has adapted its strategy to changing conditions, both for the company itself and for China as a whole.

Table 2.1 The corporate lifecycle in China – from entry to consolidation

Questions for management	Entry	Market development	Global integration
What	Leverage home market	Develop and market local products	Produce within global web
How	Wide range of instruments	Build up local organisation	Integration into global operations
Where	China in many localities	Need to get China-wide	Time to market, quality, responsiveness
HR	Language, retention	Develop pride, 'soft' knowledge	No glass ceilings
Production	Quality, delivery, costs, know-how	Strengthen value chain	Tied into global value chains
Sales	Dual strategy advisable	Get close to client, build brand	Serve global and local markets
Organisation	Establish brand, provide services to business units	Co-ordinate business unit and HQ relations	Integrate China/regional/ global operations
Ideal manager	Experienced, needs direct support from chief executive	Senior, good HQ contacts, talk to corporate barons	Senior, manage multi-dimensionality

The same questions can be asked at each stage in the process of entering, expanding and consolidating a presence in China. During each phase, the top team learns more about operating in China and brings a new set of knowledge to the answers the next time the questions are asked. And the next time the questions are asked, they bring a new set of answers.

▎ **What** are the resources we are going to draw on if we decide to enter the China market? On entry, you are likely to be exploiting your home market expertise; as you settle in you'll be adapting your product to local customer requirements; down the line, you'll be using the China location to produce for global customers.

▎ **How** are we going to enter the Chinese market, and what instrument should we chose – plain sales into the market, a joint venture, a greenfield site? Soon, we have to be building up our local organisation, then integrating it into global operations.

▌**Where** are we going to locate in this huge country, and what are the criteria we should use to choose entry method and then location for our prospective operations? Once we have decided, we'll face the challenge of growing China-wide; all along, and especially as we start facing out to the rest of the world, we'll have to be thinking time-to-market, quality, corporate responsiveness to changing conditions.

▌**Human relations:** how are we going to go about selecting and then retaining people? Nothing will work, if we don't get HR right. Making the China organisation part of the global group means raising all glass ceilings on promotions. That's a key part of your retention strategy.

▌**Production:** how do we go about ensuring quality, timely delivery, cost control and protection of our know-how? As we nestle in, we'll be strengthening our value chain. That involves us transferring knowledge, sticking to our standards, protecting our intellectual property and learning about local skills.

▌**Sales:** what do we know about the China market, what should we be selling, and to whom? We'll have to be learning about Chinese customers, the pitfalls of developing our brand, and fitting ourselves into global networks.

▌**Organisation:** how do we establish a brand, and what are our China operation relations to be relative to our business units, our product managers or our regional and global HQs?

▌**Manager's profile:** what is the profile of the ideal manager we need to run the China operation from entry through to consolidation? As the organisation in China develops, the typical profile will be evolving.

China takeaways

A mistake we made in the early days was to try and implement systems and processes that we used in other operations. Our attitude was, 'We're the number one beer company in the world, we know how to do things.' But we found our systems and processes didn't work, or it was a major headache to sort them out. We should have been finding the best way of doing things in China.

> Eric Melloul, China director of marketing, InBev

▌ Just as you must understand China, you must also understand your own organisation.

▌ The China operation must be fully integrated into the organisation as a whole.

▌ Remember that your strategy must not be a straitjacket.

▌ Learning is key to successful organisations and doubly important in China, where things change quickly and unpredictably.

▌ China is different, do not expect to measure success in China in the same way that you measure it elsewhere.

▌ Top management must lead the way in learning by doing.

▌ Remember the different requirements of the corporate lifecycle from entry to consolidation.

Next we're going to see how China's transformation makes government relations one of the first and most important things to get right when entering China, then we'll move on to the primary resource of an efficient, successful China operation, its people.

References and bibliography

Bartlett, C.A. and Ghoshal, S. (1989) *Managing Across Borders: The transnational solution*, Boston, MA: Harvard Business School Press.

Doz, Y., and Kosonen, M. (2008) *Fast Strategy: How strategic agility will help you stay ahead of the game.* Wharton School Publishing.

Ghoshal, S., and Bartlett, C.A. (1997) *The Individualized Corporation: A fundamentally new approach to management*, New York: Harper Collins.

Hoover, W.J. (2006) 'Making China your second home market: an interview with the CEO of Danfoss', *McKinsey Quarterly*, no. 1.

Penrose, E.T. (1995) *The Theory of the Growth of the Firm*, Oxford University Press, revised paperback.

Porter, M.E. (1980) *Competitive Strategy: Techniques for Analyzing Industries and Competitors*, New York: Free Press.

Prahalad, C.K., and Doz, Y.L. (1987) *The Multinational Mission: Balancing Local Demands and Global Vision*, New York Free Press.

Sull, D., with Yong Wang (2005) *Made in China: What Western Managers Can Learn from Trailblazing Chinese Entrepreneurs*, Harvard Business School Press, 25–48.

Government relations

The party-state structure means that government relations at all levels are very important.

Rob Westerhof, former chief executive, Philips Greater China

The dichotomy of what's written in the laws and what's practised in reality is really a much bigger challenge than I anticipated.

Michael Sagan, area manager, Ikea, Central China

China's government is complex and opaque. There are five levels, often with overlapping responsibilities, as often as not uncoordinated, and frequently competitive. Decision-making power is far from transparent and government initiatives affecting enterprises can be introduced without warning. The state is a customer for many companies, it is the prime investor in infrastructure and government procurement markets are huge. The state can also change markets, particularly when it introduces reform packages. Ultimately, it is the party-state rather than the market that controls businesses, using a variety of tools from tax breaks to free trade zones, and from non-tariff barriers to a market free-for-all.

Given the omnipresence, complexity and unpredictability of government, managing relationships with officialdom is crucial at all stages of business development in China. Government relations are not something you can indulge in while you're getting set up and then forget about, they will always be significant, must be cultivated continuously, and can never be taken for granted.

In this chapter, we will look at why government relations in China are so important, what makes them so complex, some of the challenges inherent in dealing with Chinese bureaucracy, and the factors upon which your government-relations strategy depends.

Why government relations are so important

It is not easy to do business in China. The World Bank's six governance indicators – voice and accountability, political stability and absence of violence, government effectiveness, regulatory quality, rule of law, and control of corruption – are based on expert indices and surveys that reflect what business people and analysts in Western and emerging markets think about business conditions in two hundred and twelve countries. It's no surprise to find that the 2007 results show China far behind the thirty countries of the Organisation for Economic Co-operation and Development (OECD). across all six indicators. For voice and accountability, China scores among the lowest at 5.8, compared with rankings in the nineties for countries such as Australia and the UK, confirming the obvious – that the party-state likes reaching decisions behind closed doors. Government effectiveness reaches the dizzy heights of 61.1. Still a lot less effective than Australia (97.2) and the UK (93.8), but the figure does imply that the government can get things done – if it wants to. Rounding up the other indicators, political stability (32.2), regulatory quality (45.6), rule of law (42.4) and control of corruption (30.9) demonstrates that China, although better than Nigeria in five out of the six (Nigeria ranks 31.7 for voice and accountability), has a long way to go before it can match Australia (78.8, 96.1, 94.8 and 94.7, respectively) or any of the other OECD countries.

Another take on the China picture for business comes from the Opacity index, which looks at corruption, legal systems, enforcement systems, accounting and disclosure standards, and regulatory quality – and covers forty-eight countries. The index is designed to explore the level of risk faced by investors going into a country. Finland has the lowest risk for foreign investors, China comes in at 41, above Brazil, Saudi Arabia, the Philippines, Colombia, Venezuela, Lebanon and Nigeria, just below India and

Pakistan, and six places below Russia. Hong Kong, ranked separately despite being part of China's 'one country, two systems', ranks second behind Finland and just above Singapore.

The higher the risk of investing in a country, the greater the expected rate of return must be to offset that risk. The greater the expected rate of return, the harder businesses must work to mitigate risk.

> By far the greatest proportion of risk that businesses face is down to the party-state

If we look at China, by far the greatest proportion of risk that businesses face is down to the party-state, not just because it controls everything, but also because it is riven by feuds, conflicts of interest and policy differences. Hence the unpredictability of just about everything that businesses need to obtain or know about – including land, energy, accounting and technical standards, tax regimes and implementation of regulations. The party-state can make or break your business. But with authorities at different levels doing apparently contradictory things, detailed knowledge about the internal bargaining and policy trade-offs that go on is essential, and that knowledge can only be obtained by keeping close to the people that matter. Let's take a look at how the system works – or doesn't.

One system, two roads

China is still ruled by the communist party (CCP) and, as one senior manager observed, 'the communist party is still communist'. The CCP has over seventy million members, controls all the levers of power, and owns the land and the financial system. A party committee oversees every party or state institution, at all levels, and the control mechanism wielded by the top leadership is a 'nomenklatura' system similar to that found in the former Soviet Union. The Soviet system was represented by a list of influential posts that could only be filled by party appointees, and a second list documenting possible candidates. In China, nomenklatura appointments number in their thousands, with one list for senior appointments to state corporations and financial institutions, and another for party-state appointments going through all levels of government.

Not surprisingly, party appointments bring status, power and opportunities for financial gain, making the incumbents and their potential successors unwilling to cede any authority, and thus working against both greater democratisation and transparency. Since these appointments are only available to CCP members and current members want to preserve their chances of advancement, joining the party is a long and difficult process, involving several rounds of evaluation, attendance at meetings and participation in party activities. Once accepted, a member has to undergo a year's probation before they can begin to think about being put on any nomenklatura lists. Despite the apparent ideological rigour of these tests, nepotism and bribery also feature in the application process, and many who persevere in joining do so for the financial and other opportunities membership will bring.

The focus of state power is made up of the National People's Congress, Presidency, State Council, Central Military Commission, Supreme People's Court and Supreme People's Procuratorate. The State Council is the highest administrative organ, and the premier is assisted by four vice-premiers, five state councillors and twenty-eight ministers. The next level is local government. China is divided administratively into four municipalities (Beijing, Chongqing, Shanghai and Tianjin), twenty-three provinces, five autonomous regions and two special administrative regions (Hong Kong and Macao). Provinces are divided into autonomous prefectures, which in turn are divided into counties, autonomous counties and cities. Autonomous regions are divided into counties and autonomous counties, which are made up of townships, ethnic townships and towns. Cities are divided into districts and counties. As well as special administrative regions, there are special economic zones, development zones, mining industrial zones and nature reserves. In addition, fifteen large cities, including Dalian, Guangzhou, Ningbo and Xian, have their economic plans listed separately in the national planning and hence have their own city governments, which are ranked as sub-provincial but are not controlled by their corresponding provincial government.

The political system employs about ten million people, to which must be added the seventy million party members, the sixty-five million people employed in state enterprises, and the 155 million employed in collective enterprises. The top leadership is composed of about thirty people, whose main control mechanism is the nomenklatura system: the party personnel department supervises two lists: one for senior appointments to state corporations and financial institutions; and the other for party-state appointments right down through the five levels of government. In addition, the party-state administrative system, despite the expansion of the market arena and the explosion of private health, housing and education, holds innumerable levers over society. To put it bluntly, all land is owned by the state, and all rights are determined by administrative decision. The CCP is omnipresent. It is definitely not doing 'fading away', as Karl Marx anticipated socialist governments would do.

The party-state in China, as in every country, has its different layers of government. But since the positions of authority in each layer are filled by party members and must answer to party orders, so at each layer the chain of command comes down through both the state institutions and the corresponding party committees. This is crucial for your business to understand. Each ministry or bureau at the centre has entities at the different territorial levels, at least down to county level. These are paralleled by party organs at the different levels. The result is a complex pattern of vertical relationships (*tiao*) and horizontal relationships (*kuai*). The term *tiaokuai guanxi*, meaning the relationships between these vertical and horizontal lines, refers to the complex issue of which authority has priority over others. A state bureau at county level, for instance, is subordinate to its local county government, which is responsible for the bureau's funding and appointment of staff; but the state bureau is also under the tutelage of its provincial government superior. All levels of the state bureaucracy have a corresponding CCP committee, which ensures that party discipline is obeyed and has the power to affect career opportunities. What is more, agreement for any action you may be seeking from the state bureau at county level has to be reached along both vertical and horizontal lines. If any official in the matrix is opposed to the proposed action, he or she can veto the project.

The all-pervasive party-state connections flow from the fact that there is no separation of powers, no independent judiciary, and, of course, no executive accountable to an elected legislature. In the longer term, there is no doubt that China is creating a legal system, which has the potential to develop as an institutional rival to the party. For the moment, though, the courts are subordinate to the party-state. At national level, the National People's Congress (NPC) – to which the courts are answerable – the State Council and provincial authorities issue a bevy of laws and regulations. These new laws borrow extensively from Western traditions, concepts and procedures – a process that has accelerated as China entered the WTO.

> Beijing comes up with all these regulations and implementation processes. Then the officials from Beijing have to go to every single city in China to train people how to implement the new regulations. Of course things get lost in translation, they get misinterpreted, and the way the law is written, it's very grey. You can interpret it any way you want. There's no black and white.
>
> Kristina Koehler, director, Klako Group, Shanghai

Within China, there is a massive judicial system of 3,000 courts and nearly 200,000 judges. But many of these judges, beyond the maritime fringe of China, are retired officials of the People's Liberation Army (PLA), who lack legal training and bring military methods into the courts. Defence lawyers run the risk of being indicted. Local judges tend to be biased to local interests, not surprisingly, as they are beholden to local party-state policy networks, and are subordinate to local people's congresses. Politics continues to prevail over law in China.

Nonetheless, there has been a huge increase in the number of lawsuits filed through China's courts. There have been three types of litigation. First, private entrepreneurs have used commercial litigation on contract law:

> A lot of what I read in the West is hype. There is a legal framework for doing business here. You need lawyers to negotiate a contract. If people break it, you can get them to a court and get your money back. Again, my experience is in Shanghai, not the

rest of China. The government here has created an environment very conducive for foreign companies to do business.

Alan Hepburn, managing director, Three on the Bund, Shanghai

Second, recourse to civil legislation has been one of the channels for citizens to air their grievances, alongside petitions, participation in elected village committees, mass demonstrations, or plain violence. According to statistics provided by the Ministry of Public Order, the number of 'mass incidents' countrywide increased from 8,700 in 1993 to 40,000 in 2000, and 87,000 in 2005 – a tenfold increase. The number of participants in the protests – staged in response to mass job losses in the cities, to illegal evictions, and other official abuses – rose from 860,000 in 1993 to 3.7 million a decade later. These 'mass incidents' were occurring across the length and breadth of China; indicated greater awareness by participants of their citizen rights; demonstrated the wide variety of backgrounds from which protestors came; and displayed a readiness to use a variety of methods from laying siege to government offices, burning officials' houses, blockading roads and rail, including appeal to the law and the courts and to central government (see box on p.67). Not least, there were clear signs that discontent was becoming organised, with the emergence of such groups as the Peasant Burden Reduction Group or the Peasant Rights Preservation Committee. Here was a direct challenge to a party that had conquered China with the support of the rural masses, and claimed a monopoly over political power.

A third has been the area of administrative legislation, where complaints have been brought against public officials. One such case has made legal history. Judge Li Huijuan, fresh from her studies, faced with a conflict between national and provincial law, declared the provincial law invalid (Yardley, 2005). This provoked the ire of the People's Congress of Henan province, which challenged the right of a local judge to override local laws. But Judge Li won the support of the Beijing Lawyers Association, which petitioned the central government on her behalf. She also made contacts at the People's Supreme Court, attracted media attention and set in motion a national debate about judicial independence. A legal conference on the subject was organised at

Tsinghua University, and in the summer of 2004, she returned to her judicial post. What this incident indicates is that there is support in Beijing for the rule of law, rather than of party officials, but it also shows that the support is embedded in a maze of central-local power battles. In other words, how much time to spend with your lawyers, and how how time to spend building relationships, depends very much on where your operations are in China.

Lack of rule of law has led to uncertainty. Local governments are permitted to interpret and implement national laws to suit their own situations. Towns, cities and regions have nationally mandated economic targets, and any law that means these targets will not be met can be conveniently ignored. For instance, a city or county may decide not to comply with rules on importing machinery if the imports help them meet targets for local income. This can help or hinder your business – after all, if you're the one wanting to import machinery such a move is a good thing. However, if it is your competitors bringing in the machines, that gives the deal a different complexion. When you operate from more than one location in China, you will find that conditions at each site will be different, with variations in the many permits, certifications, and other bureaucratic instruments necessary to start operations. It is next to impossible to unify operations and processes across China: indeed, Philips, the Dutch consumer electronics giant, was thinking about harmonising all the joint venture operations it had entered in to over the years, but came to the conclusion that the supposed benefits would not be worth the effort.

The devolution of power involves more than policies and regulations. It creates great diversity in the supply chain, with numerous internal borders that mark changes sometimes equivalent to those between countries. This means that

Distribution costs can be affected when transporting goods across provincial borders

distribution costs can be affected when transporting goods across provincial borders, and you will have to have relationships with all agencies involved.

The layers of administration are not just multifarious, their very existence implies a network of connections between them, and inevitably there are overlaps and conflicts. An infrastructure project, for instance, might need thirty approvals from different agencies, including environment, foreign investment, taxation and land administration. The problem is compounded by the fact that these agencies may have different policy goals and there may be little co-ordination between them, so one agency's reason for approval can be another agency's reason for refusal.

> The lack of transparency in decision-making is a risk, an important reason to make sure you have good relationships with local government officials.
>
> Mark Siezen, managing director, Redevco Europe

On top of this, there is China's 2001 admission to the WTO. Membership was based on China's agreement to bring its trading laws and economic environment into line with other members of the WTO. In the press release announcing the successful conclusion of fifteen years' of negotiations, Mike Moore, director-general of the WTO at the time, said of the organisation that 'the near-universal acceptance of its rules-based system will serve a pivotal role in underpinning global economic co-operation'. And companies are certainly finding that things are changing for businesses in China. WTO entry has led to formal consultative processes between the administration and business, notably foreign business interests, and trade policy cases, involving anti-dumping procedures against Chinese companies, has led such companies to hire US lawyers in their defence. But since local governments in China do not implement national laws exactly as Beijing intends them, so too must we expect that total WTO compliance may be a long time coming. There's no rush, as chief Chinese trade negotiator Long Yongtu said of the negotiations (Kirby, 2001): 'A fifteen-year process is a blink of the eye in the 5,000-year history of China.'

Part of WTO compliance involves unifying tax systems. Taxes are collected at both local and national levels, and compliance will have to overcome considerable hurdles as local authorities struggle to retain the fees they collect from businesses. Changes to the value-added tax (VAT) system, for instance, will mean shifting the payment burden from producers to consumers, and thus from local collection to national collection. Somehow, Beijing will have to find a way to comply fully with WTO rules and bring the rest of the country into line. Meanwhile, foreign companies will have to be on their toes as the changes happen.

Getting to know you

It is not easy to find who to contact in this complicated government structure. You really need a Chinese agent or partner to help. I've been here for ten years and I still don't know how to do it without making mistakes.

Gerald Kaufmann, general manager of
the Liaoning RHI Jinding Magnesia

All the companies talked to when researching this book stressed the importance of government relations, at all levels. They described why they needed to talk to officials from ministries right down to municipality and township levels, and how they went about it. Some pointed out that the wide variations mean that you must explore several locations to find the best package for your operation, but all cautioned that you should be ready for the situation to change wherever you locate. Let's hear what they had to say about the different levels of government, how they actually went about finding and meeting the right people, and the particular challenges that government relations in China present.

Since so many of your business decisions depend on official approval, you must have good relationships with all the relevant government departments. I don't think there's any environment where it is not important to have good relationships with the people who could affect your business, it is just that there is so much more in China because the state is more present in everything you do.

Fraser G. White, founder and chief executive,
Dulwich College Management International

You need to start building relationships with officials long before you establish operations. You need national and local relationships because you will need approval from the top, but it is only at the local level that you will be able to refine your calculations sufficiently to determine whether or not your China venture is a viable proposition. If you make your projections based only on national regulations and tax regimes, you are unlikely to come up with useful forecasts.

To give an example of top-down relationships, we can look at B&Q's Pudong store, which opened in 2001. Before doing so, it had sought approval from Beijing via the Ministry of Commerce and the Ministry of Foreign Trade and Economic Development. Subsequently, managers had spoken to the Shanghai municipal government and the Pudong authorities to get their approval, and finally to the officials of Huamu township, where the store was built, who were reassured that B&Q would hire local residents wherever possible. Stora Enso also needed approvals at several levels:

> For our Suzhou operation, it's very important that we have a good relationship with both the Suzhou district officials and the Suzhou city municipal officials. For our plantation in the south, we need good relationships with the top officials of Guangxi province, and also with Beijing because of the approvals we need for the whole project.
>
> Wangqiu Song, Stora Enso, China

Local governments can introduce non-tariff barriers that can keep other foreign companies out

The reason you need all these relationships was highlighted earlier – the fact that what happens locally does not necessarily match what is mandated nationally. Some of the benefits of developing good relationships with local government include advance information on policy trends at the higher levels and how these are likely to be interpreted lower down, and even preferential treatment over foreign competitors. Local governments can introduce non-tariff barriers that can keep other foreign companies out, or at least make it harder and more expensive for them to get established.

The people who implement laws at the local level have a great deal of flexibility in how they interpret those laws, and hence a lot of power. That's why it is so important to build the right relationships with local officials. Many foreign companies have problems dealing with the inconsistencies. You have to develop a different management style to cope.

Humphrey Lau, president, Novozymes, China

A note of caution here – since every location will come with its own business and tax regimes, it will be difficult to make comparisons and you will need to bring other sources of information to bear on your choice.

Be careful about responding to local government incentive packages to locate in their area. Local governments roll out the red carpet in the hope of attracting investors. They offer all types of inducements – land, tax, trade union exemptions, finance.

Rob Westerhof, former chief executive, Greater China, Philips

Getting to know the right officials can be a challenge in itself. If you are a huge, well-known company making a large investment, you may find the red carpet rolled out with alacrity, but if you are a small company or are making a relatively small investment, you may struggle to reach the people you need to meet. As Scott Kennedy has argued in his book, *The Business of Lobbying in China*, the key feature of government-business relations is the industrial sector and business you are in. Membership in trade associations – all under party-state tutelage – is standard, but the value of trade associations is greater for consumer electronics firms than it is for steelmakers. The big firms in steel have the direct ear of officialdom in Beijing, but Beijing is frustrated in its efforts to promote concentration in the industry by the construction lobbies operating at local government level. Where firms are ready to defend their interests, as is the case in the highly competitive consumer electronics sector, they can achieve political victories even when they conflict with that of government or of their competitors.

It is not only size and sector that matters, but also how much media coverage your sector gets. Steel or mining is sturdy stuff, but only interesting for media when big interests are at stake, as when in January 2005 Brazil's Companhia Vale do Rio Doce (CVRD) – one of the three suppliers with Australia's BHP Billiton and Rio Tinto to supply 80 per cent of the world's demand for iron ore – unilaterally raised iron ore prices by 71 per cent. The price rise came as a shock to Chinese steelmakers who sought, with Beijing's support, to constitute a tight oligopoly to negotiate with the three big iron ore producers. But local interests, with their 6,000-odd smaller steel producers, hungry for iron ore to meet local demand, stood in their way.

By contrast, the more glamorous and fast-moving software and consumer electronics industries attract more media coverage, helping to advertise your brand. The glamour, of course, can be affected by your country of origin as the Spanish telecommunications company Telefonica found out. Telefonica found China challenging because Spain was perceived as backward. The fact that Chinese want to learn English before any other language was also a barrier. Relationships are particularly critical in a highly regulated industry such as telecoms, and the company used Spanish government connections to establish top-level contacts in China and sponsored numerous events in their relationship-building efforts. Telefonica also works with the Spanish cultural organisation Instituto Cervantes in China to promote Spain more widely.

> We were very lucky because we started at the top with the minister. Then we established very good relationships with all the vice-ministers, and the vice-premier in charge of telecoms visited Spain. Now we are focused on the lower levels, on the people we need to deal with day to day.
>
> Ms Hong Chen Jin (Margaret Chen), alternate director, Telefonica

There are other avenues for meeting officials, such as lectures and events organised by your embassy or cultural organisation, or conferences organised by industry association and other relevant bodies. Sometimes useful contacts can even be made outside China:

On a trip back to the UK, I met a local government delegation from a district in Chengdu who were visiting the UK looking for investors. I will meet them here next week, and that will be the start of building another relationship with the local government. I find that the quickest way to get to talk to most local governments, though, is to talk to their investment departments to find out what types of foreign investment they're looking for. Then I can go straight to whoever is in charge of those particular projects.

Keith Linch, chief architect, Robinson JZFZ, China

Things change over time, as well. Companies that went into China early often had a first-mover advantage when it came to setting up government relationships, as they were among the earliest to invest in particular locations. But as foreign investment into China increased, both in total amount and in size of individual projects, it has become harder for smaller companies to maintain their status as a valued foreign investor in a town or region.

When we were first here, we were visited by the premier and the vice-premier. Nowadays, it's the lower level people who interact with us. My staff tell me that it's still good, we're interacting with the right people, we're a small company now – whereas ten years ago, ours was a huge investment, now other companies are investing much more. But I don't buy that. We should be interacting with people at the ministerial level, and I know we can do that. I'm pushing my staff to think of ways to open doors, for instance we are arranging a biofuel conference that will bring us higher contacts, and if we have to pay lobby consultants, then we'll do that. We need the relationships.

Humphrey Lau, president, Novozymes, China

Our clients coming in to China are small companies, a thousand employees maximum. If you're not investing in the millions in China, then you're not expected to meet all the top officials. Obviously, you have to contact the various departments to do all the paperwork and get the permissions, but you're not expected to do the wining and dining in the same way that multinationals are.

Kristina Koehler, director, Klako, Shanghai

Along with the challenges of finding the appropriate target ministries, agencies and people is the problem of how to approach and develop the necessary relationships. First, there will be distinctions between the people themselves. Older members of the administration are from a different era. They are often badly educated, loyal party members, speak little or no English and have a tendency to stick to the 'old ways'. Younger officials will be the result of Deng's push to 'make our cadre ranks more revolutionary, younger in average age, better educated and professionally more competent' and may well speak good English. You will have to adapt your approach depending on whom you are talking to.

Building relationships with government officials has an added dimension, the threat of death

Business relationships in China are built through the exchange of favours and over dinner and other social events, not just in the board room and on the pages of a contract. Building relationships with government officials has an added dimension, the threat of death. Corruption is a problem in China, and those found guilty of economic crimes may be executed. The former head of the Chinese State Food and Drug Administration, Zheng Xiaoyu, was executed in 2007 for receiving $825,000 in cash and gift bribes; Hu Changqing, the former vice-governor of south-central Jiangxi province was executed for taking bribes and not being able to explain the origins of $195,000-worth of property and gifts. The lower limit of such economic crimes is roughly $12,000, and anyone found guilty of accepting upwards of this amount faces a minimum of ten years in jail, with life imprisonment and execution being saved for more serious offenders. Foreign companies entering China will almost invariably have their own, home country laws on corruption to deal with, too, and so you are advised to tread carefully.

Nevertheless, foreign companies are expected to contribute to individuals and the local community in ways not normally seen on the balance sheet. You may be invited to make an ad hoc contribution to a local infrastructure project, such as new drains, and find that permits are much easier to come by after this contribution has been made. You will be expected to ease the social care burden of the local administration by providing housing and medical subsidies to your employees, and perhaps the poorer families in the area as well. A contact may recommend someone as a suitable adviser or consultant and you would be wise to consider their suggestion seriously, while remaining wary of taking such people on board. At a more prosaic level, a company car may be needed for lifts to important functions, or your product might be offered for sale at a discount to local purchasers.

There is no way round this. Officials have the power to stop or start a business with no warning, and any company thought to be not playing the game can find itself beset by inspections (there are at least sixty government agencies that are permitted by law to visit a business at any time) or smothered in red tape. So many things in China are resolved through 'informal authority' rather than through the law, that any company without the necessary relationships can find it almost impossible to do business.

What to do if your business model becomes illegal

US direct-selling company Amway was forced to rethink its Chinese business model when it suddenly found itself operating illegally in 1998. Without warning, the government banned all direct-selling operations, deeming them fronts for pyramid selling, secret cults and other groups dangerous to society. Amway had been established in China for three years, and had recently invested $100 million in a factory in Guangzhou and eight distribution centres. It was also planning a $25–30 million investment in Shanghai when it found its China operations illegal and its stock price plummeting back home.

The company instantly instigated high-level communications with government officials and remarkably, after only three months, secured an agreement that would allow Amway to start trading again. The company was obliged to open shops, which cost it $29 million and remain unique in its global operations, and sign labour contracts with its salespeople. By 2002, the new model was proving so successful that Amway sales in China reached $700 million, roughly four times what they had been before the direct-selling ban.

'We've been told to shut down five times and to change our way of doing business four times,' Eva Cheng, chairman of Amway China, pointed out in September 2005. Clearly, having to adapt has helped – China is one of Amway's most important markets.

Good relationships with the appropriate officials can make an enormous difference. US company Butler Builders was given a great deal of advice on permits, licensing requirements and local construction regulations by officials in the Songjiang industrial zone, which helped get its operation up and running. Other companies have been able to find novel solutions to unexpected tax and other bills, understanding not only that all charges are open to negotiation, but also that simply taking the right person out to dinner might be all that's necessary for a mutually acceptable outcome. Even fines can be treated in this way.

There is another aspect to building relationships with Chinese officials – many of them appear to be averse to risk and avoid making decisions. This can be due to several causes. Sometimes, you may be negotiating with the wrong person, who does not have the power to decide but is unable to tell you this, as both you and they will lose face. At other times, it is the very fact of deciding that is difficult, because once a decision has been made, someone has to take responsibility for the outcomes. In addition, some bureaucrats make no effort to communicate with business, and others duplicate activities or compete with other departments. Overlap between departments can be difficult to spot, and dealing with it when you do find it can be tricky. Sometimes it is up to you to take the initiative, by finding a way to obtain a decision without anyone actually deciding.

It is well to bear in mind that many of the problems you perceive as a foreign company dealing with Chinese bureaucracy are not necessarily about you. Chinese companies face the same sudden changes and unforeseen tax charges, they too have to negotiate the ever-confusing corridors of power to get the right permits and chops. They may have an advantage in that they will be better connected and perhaps quicker at finding the decision-maker, but they may not be able to offer the same financial support to local society as you. And while you see dealing with the administration as a great burden on your time and resources, the officials will probably see you in a similar light, you're foreign so you don't understand, you probably won't be around long and another foreigner who knows even less will come to take your place, and there's no point trying to build a relationship with someone who isn't committed to China. You will be their 'blink of an eye'.

> There's no point trying to build a relationship with someone who isn't committed to China

The state as customer

Government is one of your key targets when building a brand in China.

Scott Kronick, president, Ogilvy, China

Some experienced China hands recommend treating the state as your most important customer. In some industry sectors, such as engineering design and architecture, the state will literally be your biggest customer, for other sectors, especially those that are highly regulated, state influence will be of strategic significance.

At the moment, there's a huge debate within the Chinese government about how to reform healthcare. The biggest challenge for the development of healthcare as an industry in China is when and at what point market mechanisms will be allowed to develop either on the customer side or the provider side. My guess is that there are a lot of industries and a lot of other sectors in China in the same situation. The role of the state as customer or provider must be understood.

Kabir Nath, president, Bristol-Myers Squibb, China

Companies who sell to government must have relationships that enable them to operate as a business and relationships that are all about the work that they do.

Our government relationships are extremely important, particularly those with the Ministry of Construction, because of the nature of our [architectural] work and the fact that we need special approvals for big projects. For each project, the ministry puts together a panel of experts and they work with the design team towards getting approval. We spent over a year and a half in dialogue for the CCTV project, literally hundreds of meetings, formal and informal. It's a good process because it's based on engineering requirements and we develop jointly a very clear and detailed set of criteria for every aspect of the project.

Rory McGowan, Arup

Government also affects markets. New regulations can cause rapid shifts in the way that markets develop, and cause markets to appear almost overnight.

Home ownership is a good example of how fast things are going. A little over twenty years ago, it was illegal to own your own home, the state owned all the property. Today, something like 65 per cent of homes in Shanghai are owned by individuals – that is an enormous cultural leap. It probably took us hundreds of years to get the same level of ownership in the UK; the Chinese did it in twenty years.

Steve Gilman, B&Q

Not least, government is important to you because of what third parties to the relationship can mean to your business. According to the US Department of State Report on Human Rights, there were 317,000 registered non-governmental organisations (NGOS) operating in China in 2006. The report adds that registered and unregistered quasi-governmental organisations and NGOs operating in China may number as many as eight million. Given the interdependence between China and developed world markets, associations and NGOs operating in the US and the EU would have to be added to the organisations that exert a direct or indirect influence on government and business policies. What that means for your business activities in China is that you will be operating in a goldfish bowl as far as your visibility back home is concerned. You have to conceive of your corporation's future there as conditioning your brand and reputation in your home market.

While on the subject of third parties, it is as well to bear in mind, too, that in China's highly fractious policy arena, civil society has also been strengthened in its relations to the nominally monolithic party-state by the internet. The party-state has sought to control its development, as discussed in the previous chapter, but remains vulnerable to online petitions that appeal to anti-foreigner, particularly anti-Japanese, sentiments which the party-state has fostered to promote a sense of Chinese nationalism. Since the 1990s, greater freedoms for Chinese historians has led to a rise in the number of professional articles about Japanese activities in the Sino-Japanese wars of 1931–45. An online campaign waged by nationalists in July 2003 obliged the government to backtrack on a $12 billion contract to Japan for the building of the Beijing-Shanghai high-speed rail link. A petition, which gathered thirty million signatures in April 2005, pressed the government to state more clearly its opposition to Japan's bid to acquire a permanent UN Security Council seat. The party-state cannot afford to ignore its own public opinion, any more than you can afford to ignore public opinion at home.

Government relations as strategy

Keeping track of who holds the political power is a constant demand of doing business in China. Without a carefully considered government relations programme, you won't have a China strategy. You need to adopt a multi-pronged approach, through direct relationships with authorities, using Chinese and foreign lobbying and public relations firms, and by participating in business associations and other industry activities. How you develop this element of your strategy will depend on factors such as the industry sector you operate in, the characteristics of your particular market, how important China is to global operations and company size.

Some sectors have special exemptions under the WTO agreement and are still protected by the Chinese government, whereas for others, foreign companies may be encouraged, typically in the form of financial and other operational incentives. If the market for your products is highly regulated, you will need strong relationships with the officials who determine and implement the regulations. If your market is highly competitive, good relationships with government may help you to achieve acceptable margins. Good government relations can also make day-to-day operational life smoother.

Our relationships with government are helped by the fact that we pay a lot of attention to details. We make sure we get the paperwork right, for instance for importing goods, and this demonstrates that our administration is efficient. We also have an extremely good safety record, with zero accidents at our Wuqing factory, which shows local government that we are a good employer. We also demonstrate that we treat our staff properly through the benefits we provide, such as medical insurance and pension contributions. The authorities see that we are efficient, conscientious and fair, and we get fewer random checks as a result.

Niels-Erik Olsen, vice-president, Danfoss China

So how do you choose the right strategy for dealing with government relations in China? Let's look at four possibilities and the factors that help you to decide between them.

The first approach would be to avoid trouble by not going into China at all, or to establish a limited commitment that is just enough to keep your options open. A limited commitment would still involve government relations, but if you are not building a factory or employing people directly, the relationships can be much less complicated. The advantage of this strategy for the organisation is that you don't have to cope with the long march to profitability, which has been the lot of many companies setting up in China. The few statistics available show that returns are very much higher elsewhere, and China could be a drain on an otherwise successful business.

A second option emerges if the expected significance of the China market to your company is high but your bargaining power is low, for instance if your company is smaller or has low brand recognition.

Smaller companies find it harder to meet high-ranking government officials

Smaller companies with low bargaining power find it harder to meet high-ranking government officials because they have less money to invest and do not enhance the officials' status sufficiently. Here, your strategy would be to go along with local government demands, adapting to meet their requirements.

In this case, location and, if applicable, choice of partner is absolutely crucial because, as discussed above, local government sets the rules. Specialist consultants with a track record in this type of location issue are getting easier to find and you are strongly advised to use their services. You can enhance your lobbying power in two ways, either as part of an industry group – strength in numbers – or through your embassy or consulate, which puts negotiations on a government-to-government footing and therefore gives them greater political significance.

Conversely, if the expected significance of the China market is rather low and your bargaining power is high – you represent a significant investment and a well-known brand, an opportunistic approach may pay dividends. Top management could adopt a 'let's see' attitude, with the proviso that any China operations do not detract from more important markets elsewhere. Local governments in China gain face if a big-name company locates in their city or region, and have investment targets to meet, which could create interesting opportunities. A visit by an important foreign managing director can open all sorts of doors.

Finally, when market significance and bargaining power are both high, then you are in a position to challenge local demands and negotiate concessions with public officials. This has been Alcatel's strategy. In 2002, the French telecoms company created a unique operation when it consolidated more than a dozen Chinese joint ventures into Alcatel Shanghai Bell. The highly regulated telecoms industry in China was a hard nut to crack, but Alcatel's deal meant that they retained control, having 50 per cent plus one share and the government owning the rest. Part of the arrangement was that Alcatel moved its regional headquarters to Shanghai, showing the strength of its commitment to China, and a logical step for a company that considered China to be one of its biggest markets.

The readiness is all...

Hank Greenberg, chief executive of US insurance company AIG, devoted seventeen years to building relationships with central and provincial government officials in China so that when the Chinese insurance market was opened up to foreign companies, AIG was first in the door and other companies were locked out.

China takeaways

Whatever your situation, government relations will be fundamental to your China operation so you must make them a core part of your business strategy. Adopting this attitude from the start will go a long way towards making your relationships with officials productive and beneficial.

▌ Remember that you cannot turn government relations on and off – a consistent, metholodical approach is necessary. You have to build up relationships over time.

▌ Use all means at your disposal to make contacts with officialdom at all levels. Don't fear the government – it can often be helpful.

▌ Remember that high-level officials will expect to meet equally senior members of your company.

▌ Do not assume that national laws will be implemented in full where your China operation is located.

▌ Be patient 1: the lack of transparency makes even finding out the simplest thing time-consuming.

▌ Be patient 2: provide all the information you are asked for, however insignificant it may seem, and don't be surprised if you have to provide the same information several times to different agencies.

▌ Do not assume that once you've set up in China, you can put government relations to one side – continuing dialogue with the authorities must be part of operations.

▌ In China, you operate in a goldfish bowl as far as public opinion is concerned at home.

China's transformation, your organisation and how these combine in a critical way with each layer of government create a big-picture view of what you are letting yourself in for. Now it's time to start looking at the China operation in more detail, and your primary choices – business structure, location and timing. Then we'll move on to the backbone of your China operation, the people.

References and bibliography

Deng, X. (1982–1992) *Selected Works of Deng Xiaoping* vol. 3, Foreign Languages Press, Beijing.

Kirby, J. (2001) 'China enters WTO fold', 17 September BBC News website, http://news.bbc.co.uk/1/hi/business/1548866.stm.

Yardley, J. (2005) 'A young judge tests China's legal system', *International herald Tribune*, 29 November.

China choices: business structure and location

There are plenty of choices once you start exploring how and where to set up your China operations. As you have already learnt, the regulatory environment for your business may vary according to where you operate, so you need to investigate locations thoroughly. But location choices also have to include decisions about what sort of business structure you are going to establish. If you're only thinking of selling via an agent based in Hong Kong, you hardly need to investigate the legal ramifications of doing business in Wuhan.

There is much conflicting advice about which business structure is best. Some say to avoid joint ventures (JV) at all costs, while others believe foreign companies must work with local partners to gain market access and understand customer needs. There is certainly a high failure rate for JVs, but many of the people interviewed for this book understand that such ventures can work, as long as you put sufficient effort into setting them up. Sometimes, JVs are the only way to access the market. Clearly defining your strategic requirements will go a long way towards helping you identify the best entry mode. Let's start with another big picture – the reason why there are so many ways of doing business in China.

An ever-widening door

China's growth has gone hand in hand with a rapid evolution in policy, so that a variety of routes to enter the China market have evolved. This trial-and-error approach to foreign investment was partly due to what China permitted, and partly due to how foreign firms viewed China.

In the early 1980s, multinationals treated China much like other developing countries – as places to sell old products or as locations for the manufacture and distribution of old technologies. Because they knew little about the country, they often proceeded tentatively. The party-state behaved no differently. As was to be expected, laws and regulations were restrictive. A primary goal was to protect public ownership, but sufficient incentives had to be provided so that local firms could absorb Western technologies and know-how. Thus was born the joint venture, the party-state's preferred vehicle for attracting foreign investors and tapping into their technologies. A July 1979 law (see box below) stipulated that foreign capital must account for at least a quarter of the total capital of a JV.

Realising that corporations would only start to transfer technologies to China if they could be assured of some control over operations, Beijing widened the entry option in 1986 to full foreign ownership. Further adaptations came in 1988 when laws provided a more complete legal framework for foreign corporations, protection against expropriations, access to local markets and a distribution of profits no longer dependable on partners' stakes. This co-operative form of JV became popular among Hong Kong investors in the 1990s, accounting on average for about a fifth of annual inward investments.

In 1993, the holding company formula received official sanction, allowing corporations to start using it as a mechanism for integrating their activities China-wide. This formula, together with the wholly owned option, proved attractive for multinationals, which came to replace overseas Chinese as the prime investors in China. In the following decade, the big event was China's accelerated entry to the WTO, and the adoption of global norms in the treatment of foreign investors.

The big event was China's accelerated entry to the WTO

The interaction between evolving public policy and collective corporate learning can be traced through the distribution of inward

China's foreign direct investment (FDI) regime is codified

1979 Law on joint ventures using Chinese and foreign investment.

1982 Revised constitution authorises FDI in China.

1983 Regulations for implementation of the 1979 law provided more details on operations and preferential policies for JVs. Also law to protect trade-marks.

1984 Law on patents. China starts signing agreements to avoid double-taxation with trade partners. This leads to subscribing to international agreements in respect of intellectual property rights.

1985 Law on contracts with foreign enterprises.

1986 Law on enterprises operated exclusively with foreign capital permitted the establishment of wholly foreign-owned enterprises in SEZs (special economic zones).

State Council notice on incentives to foster FDI using advanced technologies, and for exports. Later codified in the 1988 co-operative JV law.

1990 Amendments to the 1983 and 1986 laws, notably that the chairman of the board of a JV does not have to be appointed by Chinese investors. Protection provided from nationalisation.

1993 Law on unfair competition, on holding company formula.

1994 Tax provisions to unify – gradually – the treatment of domestic enterprises and FFEs. Standard 33 per cent corporate income tax and in designated cities; 18 per cent in SEZs and technology development zones. Chinese organisations able to list as joint stock companies.

1995 Interim provisions in guiding FDI (revised 1997, and in 2002) classified FDI into four categories. Projects are **encouraged** and **permitted** in designated industries that introduce new and advanced technologies, expand export capacity, raise product quality, and use local resources in central and western regions. **Restricted** and **prohibited** are projects in designated areas that make use of existing technologies, compete with domestic production or state monopolies, make extensive use of scarce resources, or are considered a danger to national safety and the environment (examples include airports, nuclear power plants, oil and gas pipelines, underground systems and railways, water projects, aerospace, cars, defence, hi-tech vaccines, mining, printing, shipping, satellite communications, tourism).

2000 Regulation permitting individuals to sign franchise contracts with foreign corporations.

2001 WTO commitments include non-discriminatory treatment of foreign and domestic enterprises, rules on intellectual property rights, elimination of requirements on FDI such as foreign exchange, technology transfer, local content, export performance. Sectoral commitments include national treatment for foreign firms, ending geographic and other restrictions on cars, telecommunications, life insurance, banking and distribution, and personnel, though the pay-off comes in terms of proximity to the market, listening to customers and taking on local competition.

investment by sector and by geography. On a sectoral basis, the bulk in the early 1980s went to geological exploration – reflecting the government's hopes for energy self-sufficiency – and to real estate and tourism. Following the regulatory changes in 1986, FDI inflows shifted to export-oriented industries. Since the surge in 1993, the largest proportion has gone into manufacturing, with about half being directed to labour-intensive industries such as textiles and clothing, and the other half split equally between technology-intensive activities, such as pharmaceuticals, and capital-intensive operations, such as petroleum refining and chemicals materials. Further market opening, and China's entry to the WTO, has prompted a wave of investment in financial services. The world's leading investment banks kept a presence in Hong Kong, an ear to the floor in Beijing, and often a joint venture partnership with one of the Chinese banks.

In terms of geographic distribution, the FDI pattern reveals great disparities. The eastern region, for instance, holds nearly two-thirds of GDP and takes up 88 per cent of FDI. This, too, is largely policy driven, as the early open-door policies resulted in much of FDI bunching along the eastern coast. Most inland provinces are more closed economies, though that is changing as the interior is being opened up for development as the infrastructure boom – launched in 1998 as part of the anti-cyclical strategy to counter the effects of the

Asian financial crash – is rolled out from the coastline, to the north, the centre, to the west and to the south-west. There are many mega-projects, such as the Three Gorges Dam, the Go West strategy, the development of the Pudong business zone in Shanghai, and the creation of growth hubs around the Yangtse delta, the Pearl river delta and the Bohai Sea region. What this spells for foreign investors is the prospect of greatly improved infrastructure, the more complete integration of provincial markets across China, and a reduction in operating costs.

The interaction between evolving public policy and a collective corporate learning process about how to operate in China is illustrated in Figure 4.1. The horizontal axis traces the widening of options available to foreign investors as public policy changes, while the vertical axis traces the prospective significance of China to the company top management. On the right-hand horizontal planes are the questions that the top management team must consider: what is the country's profile? If we decide to go in, how much managerial time and effort is this likely to take, relative to other projects? What are the expected costs and benefits? What entry mode are we going to adopt? And, last but not least, what location are we going to chose?

Since China's entry to the WTO, investors may chose from a range of entry modes, from opening up a wholly owned operation to licensing their technology to locals, or just dipping their collective toe in Chinese waters to test the temperature.

Business structure options

A wholly foreign owned enterprise is definitely a lot easier to run, because you don't have to deal with a Chinese partner, but having said that, a Chinese partner can be very useful. The problem is, it's difficult to know before you start which is going to work out best of you. Hindsight is a wonderful thing.

Bill Thompson, chief executive, InBulk Technologies and executive director, Clyde Blowers, China

FIGURE 4.1 Evolution of entry mode to China markers

Companies can set up operations in China via various routes, including:

▌ representative office;

▌ agent;

▌ licensing and contract manufacturing arrangements;

▌ joint venture;

▌ wholly foreign owned enterprise (WFOE);

▌ foreign-invested stock limited company (FISLC);

▌ holding company;

▌ foreign-invested commercial enterprise (FICE) ;

▌ international procurement office.

There is room for flexibility. Some companies start initial operations under a JV, and then revert to WFOE status, others operate as a WFOE under a JV umbrella. Austrian engineering company RHI has both JVs and a WFOE, choosing the arrangement that is most appropriate to the strategic needs of each part of the organisation. No two JVs for RHI are the same, the arrangements depending on the motivation behind the venture and the relationships between senior managers.

Guala Closures used various business models to test the waters before taking the plunge

1996 Started selling in China

1997 Established relationship with agent in Hong Kong for Chinese market

1998 Set up representative office in Beijing, ended relationship with Hong Kong agent

2001 Decided to invest in setting up plant in China to gain early mover advantage

2002 Started production in China

Chinese culture places great importance on *guanxi* (see box below). Your venture in China could succeed or fail depending on how you access and use *guanxi*, and this must be taken into account as you consider which business format to adopt. Some of the methods of entering China allow you to tap into more extensive networks from the outset, others require a longer period for you to grow the connections that you will need. Above all, remember that your choice of business structure is not a strategy, it is the best tool to help you realise your China strategy.

Guanxi

Guanxi is the peculiarly Chinese blend of formal and informal, social and official relationship-building that many Westerners mistakenly liken to business networking. *Guanxi* is an important part of your business strategy in China and must be treated as such. There are many definitions, but they all boil down to personal relationships, and ultimately treating people with respect. Don't assume that *guanxi* is just about banquets and gifts, as 'meat and wine' friends are not trusted. And don't delegate, you cannot create an interpersonal relationship through a deputy.

Representative office

A representative office is set up purely for liaison purposes, it cannot earn income or make a profit, nor can it pay suppliers, and is taxed on an expenses sheet.

A representative office cannot earn income or make a profit

Permitted activities include research and information, introducing buyers and sellers through meetings, providing relevant product information to potential Chinese customers, making arrangements for visits to China and providing a co-ordinating role between the parent company and others. In theory, the parent company sends money, which the representative office uses to pay rent, travel and other expenses, but often these are charged directly to the expatriate boss's foreign credit card, so they are charged through head office, reducing the amount of tax paid in China.

It is relatively quick to set up a representative office, but a clampdown on companies having 'virtual' representative offices in Shanghai has seen new requirements imposed. Landlords renting space to representative offices have to provide proof that the company is operating at that address. The tax bureau also has to visit the company in situ before operations can start, to check how many people are working there and so estimate what should be reported on the company expense sheet. The minimum number of staff is one, but there is no upper limit to the number of people working in a representative office, nor is there any stipulation on Chinese employees, so all staff can be foreign.

Agent

If selling in China is your goal, then a simple way to start and an opportunity to test the market is through an agent. The right agent brings experience, contacts and local knowledge to the arrangement, and will represent your company in China. Not surprisingly, it is important to choose wisely. Don't assume that, because it's China, things are done differently – just as with choosing an agent anywhere else, you will need to check the agency against a list of criteria, including their credentials, the experience and qualifications of their salespeople, geographic reach and bank references. You will have to put time and resources into the relationship with your agent, with senior management visiting as frequently as possible to demonstrate the importance of the arrangement. You may have to be considerably more hands-on than you would expect elsewhere, helping to develop sales and marketing plans and training sales and after-sales staff.

Licensing and contract manufacturing

Licensing and contract manufacturing arrangements tend to be short term and set up in response to cost and managerial control requirements. No equity is involved and the relationship is theoretically straightforward, but there can be issues with product quality and delivery, and foreign companies should understand that, if things go wrong, relying on the courts to enforce this kind of business arrangement is problematic. As the China-Britain Business Council puts it, 'Most Western companies outsourcing production to China eventually find solutions and emerge from the process with satisfactory products manufactured at attractive prices,' and it is the word 'eventually' that you must be prepared for. It takes time to negotiate agreements, and even more time to ensure that quality standards can and are being met.

There are foreign companies that operate in China as intermediaries, which can take away the headache of setting up a manufacturing arrangement directly. Referred to as 'managed outsourcing', this approach gives you the added benefit not only of working with a company whose record you can check, but also of having contracts and payments arranged outside China, thus avoiding the complicated and lengthy process of direct contractual negotiations with a Chinese supplier.

Another advantage of manufacturing through a foreign contractor in China is protection of intellectual property. Components can be made in several places and assembled in a different location under supervised conditions, to minimise the number of people who see the final product.

Joint venture

> The best partner is one who shares the same dreams but not the
> same bed.
>
> Chinese saying

I have yet to read a book about business in China that does not
feature the saying about partners dreaming the same dreams in
different beds. Every author quotes it because it encapsulates the JV
dilemma. For dreams read objectives – many companies have been
surprised to find that their partner has completely different
objectives to their own. It is generally accepted that as many as
seven out of ten JVs in China fail.

> We put a lot of effort into getting what we thought was the right
> arrangement to start with. And then we changed it quickly when
> we realised that some of our original assumptions about ownership
> were wrong. We started as a 50–50 joint venture, because we
> thought that the Chinese partner would work harder to make the
> joint venture work if they owned half of it, but then we switched to
> 75–25 when we found it hard to get key decisions made.
>
> Keith Linch, chief architect, Robinson JZFZ China

The right partner can be very useful, but there are pros and cons,
and the high failure rate suggests that JVs are extremely difficult to
get right.

> ## The high failure rate suggests that JVs are
> ## extremely difficult to get right

On the plus side, a partner will bring local knowledge, the all-
important *guanxi*, market access, more economical resources, and
perhaps unique competencies. They will expect you to bring
managerial skills, financial assets, technical capabilities, and a
willingness to share your expertise. On the downside, these
expectations may be more than you are prepared to meet. It is also
easier to run your own company without a partner.

You must think about what you know and what can you find out or
develop for yourself, and balance that against the benefits a partner

can bring. A company planning to use China simply for production and then exporting all the goods is probably better off avoiding the JV structure so they have the flexibility to respond quickly to overseas customers' needs and do not have to manage a Chinese partner – who will also want a share in the profits. JVs are better for companies planning to sell in China, as the companies in the JV can develop products for the Chinese market and grow together.

> There's a very good case for foreign enterprises to work with local enterprises, because [the locals] know the market, they know the products, they know what the customers want. The foreign enterprise brings the technology, sourcing efficiencies, operational efficiencies, new skills. So if you can merge these two together, you have a huge advantage. But that requires tremendous communication and complete understanding both culturally and in the business sense. Foreign companies tend to think that only their way is the right way, and this gets in the way of good collaboration.

> Jagdish Acharya, vice-president Berger Paints, China

It takes considerable time to set up a joint venture and you must be prepared to invest this time if your JV is to be successful. Choice of partner is critical. You will have to decide on the criteria for choosing a Chinese partner and weight the different criteria according to their importance. You will then have to identify potential partners and come up with a shortlist against your selection criteria.

Criteria for choosing a JV partner

Your strategy will determine what elements you are looking for in a partner, and how important those elements are. Strategic, organisational and functional factors should be considered:

- compatible objectives;
- good management team;
- experience with foreign language companies;
- quality standards;
- R&D capability;

- location;
- support from local authorities;
- good *guanxi*;
- existing customer base;
- profitability;
- access to raw materials or components;
- access to capital;
- compliance with tax, environment and other regulations;
- adaptability and flexibility;
- willingness to learn.

Once you have a shortlist of potential partners, you have to spend time getting to know them. The viability of your JV will depend on how well the relationships function within it. Build relationships through frequent formal and informal interactions with both high- and mid-level managers from short-listed companies. Try to make surprise visits to get a sense of the company when it is not expecting you and therefore in its 'natural' state. Explore the management team's awareness of market demands and the profitability of their product lines, and, if the company has participated in a JV, find out about the results. Some companies recommend actually staying at the potential partner's location for up to two months to get to know them, arguing that the more usual habit of making several short visits prevents any in-depth understanding. Be patient, Bajaj Auto of India is still looking for a Chinese partner to help launch its motorcycles and auto rickshaws after three years, searching for a company with the same dreams of long-term growth and quality. They realise that entering China with the wrong partner is potentially more damaging than not entering China at all.

If physical assets such as land or buildings are included as part of the JV, make sure you get an independent valuation of their worth, as inflated values have often been used to try and extract greater contributions from the foreign side. While you might expect the JV to be a pooling of resources, the Chinese side is more likely to expect to set up a different company under the JV.

Diary of a joint venture for RHI

December 2004	First meeting with eventual JV partner by chance. Happened to be visiting companies nearby and assistant suggested visiting this one as well. Good first impression of general manager, decided to send in technician to assess.
May 2005	Technical assessment in, looked promising. Started to assess costs, including level of investment, savings that setting up own production would bring.
July 2005	Possible business concept presented to potential partner.
October 2005	End of negotiations on business concept, agreement in principle to terms of deal, investments by both sides, profit share to each partner, structure of JV, composition of board, who would manage.
November 2005	First draft of contract, start of next round of negotiations.
March 2006	First contract signed. One sticking point was choice of arbitrators should there be problems. RHI wanted to appoint arbitrators in Stockholm (RHI home country is Austria), JV partner wanted Chinese arbitrators in Beijing. Compromise was to nominate three arbitrators, each partner to choose the nationality of one, and the nationality of the third, who would be the main arbitrator, to be neither Austrian nor Chinese.
September 2006	Second contract signed. Many changes made, for instance because land selected by JV partner not suitable (couldn't meet environmental regulations for waste water and up a mountain, which was dangerous for transporting the fuel they would need).
January 2007	Business licence and all necessary approvals obtained.
April 2007	Construction of plant begins.

A critical aspect is control. Equity share is cited as a major factor in the strategic control of JVs, and equity of 67 per cent or more is recommended. Control over board and management appointments should confer operational control, as will leveraging non-capital resources such as technical expertise and global service support. But you must realise that equity control does not guarantee operational control. If 99 per cent of the staff are Chinese, herding cats may be easier than getting them to do what you want.

It takes time to find a partner, and perhaps even more time to negotiate the deal. One lawyer described a contract negotiation process that took five years and saw several changes of personnel in the two fifteen-strong negotiating teams.

Negotiation tips

▌ Make sure you are negotiating with the decision-maker, rather than subordinates who will have to report back.

▌ Allow a considerable amount of time, many deals are ruined by rushing. Allow for breaks, useful for cooling off or for debriefing your own team.

▌ Remember that the legal backgrounds of both sides are probably very different and adjust accordingly.

▌ Since it will be a long process, document agreements as you go along with memoranda of understanding, so that you don't have to go over old ground.

▌ Take your own interpreter.

▌ Don't get angry or flustered – self-control is essential.

▌ Consider using an advisor – they can often 'sound out' potential partner attitudes, in particular, on sensitive matters.

A word about contracts

For a Westerner, a contract is a contract, but in China it is a snapshot of a set of arrangements that happened to exist at one time.

Tim Clissold, Mr China

You can spend months, even years, negotiating contracts in China, and then find that once signed, the contract is put in a drawer and never looked at again. The absence of the rule of law makes contracts hard to enforce, which is why *guanxi* and face were, and in many cases still are, the glues that bind business arrangements together. Of course, you have to have the documents, to satisfy the shareholders back home if nothing else, but put at least as much effort into the relationships because the contract may or may not be worth the paper it is written on, depending on where you are locating in China.

Wholly foreign-owned enterprise (WFOE)

I have advised over eighty clients in the last four years. Only three have formed joint ventures, and there were strong reasons why a joint venture was best for each one. If you can avoid a joint venture, do so. That doesn't mean you won't have problems, but you won't have to get approval from a Chinese partner every time you need to make changes or implement new ideas, and this is important – because if you want to get ahead in China, you have to move fast.

Kristina Koehler, director, Klako, Shanghai

A WFOE permits you to pursue your own strategy, in line with global operations, without having to manage the perhaps different strategic objectives of a Chinese partner. WFOEs can issue invoices and receive payments in renminbi, and remit payments in foreign currencies to the parent company. A WFOE also provides better protection for intellectual property and technology.

> A WFOE provides better protection for intellectual property and technology

It's relatively simple to start up a small, wholly owned company these days. You need a minimum registered capital of $150,000, but you don't have to inject all of that in one go, we started with 15 per cent, $22,500. You have to go around about eleven different offices to register your company, national tax bureau, local tax bureau, labour, industry, all sorts of places. You can get a local agent to help get your application forms stamped by all the right people. It only took us about three months to get a WFOE started.

Bill Thompson, Clyde Blowers

Typically set up for manufacturing or assembly for export, and often located in special economic zones to take advantage of tax and other incentives, WFOEs now benefit from the freedom to trade within China itself. The Chinese government, however, controls the sectors within which foreign investors can establish WFOEs, with some sectors being closed to foreign companies, some restricted and others encouraged. Your chances of succeeding in setting up a WFOE, and obtaining the best terms for tax and VAT, are much greater if you are in an 'encouraged' sector.

While many foreign companies have chosen the WFOE route, the flexibility and control that such an arrangement offers comes at a price. Not having a partner reduces the initial costs and resources involved in setting up, and control is complete. The downside is that you will have to build all the relationships essential to business in China yourself, without the aid of a business partner who is already connected, and find your own way through the maze of administration, permits and licences before you can start operations. There is a tendency for local governments to support state-owned enterprises in preference to foreign-owned enterprises. You must build in the extra time that relationship-building will take to overcome that, and then be prepared for similar difficulties in winning customers.

The procedure for setting up a WFOE includes defining the scope of the business on the licence, and it is important to cover present and possible future activities in describing this, because a WFOE cannot conduct business outside what has been approved and licensed.

Foreign-invested stock limited company (FISLC)

Occupying a place in between the JV and the WFOE is the joint-share company structure permitted under the Sino-Foreign Invested Equity Joint Venture Law. Although this law was adopted in 1979, it was not until Kodak, the US imaging company, saw the FISLC as its only option nearly two decades later that any foreign company attempted to apply the law. The FISLC appeared to avoid the problems of control that a dysfunctional JV can bring, while addressing the WFOE's lack of contacts, *guanxi* and market access since local minority shareholders, whether companies or government investment bodies, have a vested interest in promoting and supporting the operation.

The 'Kodak clause'

It took more than four years of negotiation with the Ministry of Chemical Industry, the Ministry of Internal Trade, the Ministry of Light Industry, the Ministry of Machine Industry, the State Economic and Trade Commission, the Ministry of Foreign Trade and Economic Co-operation, the State Planning and Development Commission, four provincial governments, seven companies and others(!), the blessing of vice-premier Zhu Rongji, and a promise to invest over $1 billion before Eastman Kodak could announce that it had found a way forward in China in 1998.

Kodak wanted to restructure its Chinese investments to gain more control and build a local manufacturing, marketing and distribution base that did not require a new JV or WFOE to be set up for each additional market. They were looking for the best of both worlds, a way in which both Kodak and Chinese partners could participate, but which gave Kodak control and management flexibility.

In 1998, two companies were created, Kodak (China) Co Ltd and Kodak (Wuxi) Co Ltd, in which Kodak as parent company held 80 per cent and 70 per cent of shares, respectively. Kodak purchased the assets of two Chinese companies, Xiamen Fuda and Shantou Era, for $380 million to set up Kodak (China). The two Chinese companies received 10 per cent stakes in Kodak (China) and one seat each on the ten-member board. Since the law stipulated five shareholders, two local investment trust organisations were allocated minimal stakes.

Perhaps best of all, the deal included the agreement that no other foreign investors could enter the photographic film industry in China for three years.

Holding company

The holding company format is essentially another type of joint stock company, where the foreign investor holds the majority of the shares and retains overall management control, while the local partners receive their shares in exchange for assets. A holding company can be recognised as the regional headquarters of a multinational company and can be used to consolidate China operations. Setting up a holding company in Hong Kong before entering the China market protects the parent company overseas from retrospective application of new tax regulations, which can be an important consideration as the fluid nature of the tax environment means that companies can set up under one set of regulations but find themselves taxed under another when they start to make a profit. JVs and WFOEs that have been profitable for three years can convert to a holding company, which gives greater flexibility and opportunities to extend manufacturing and marketing operations.

Foreign-invested commercial enterprise (FICE)

Foreign investors were finally able to enter the trading and distribution sectors directly in December 2004 under WTO accession agreements. Before then, they had to sell their products through Chinese import and export companies, or via a trading company in a free-trade zone. The specifications for setting up a FICE are less onerous than those for a WFOE, including more reasonable minimum capital requirements. A FICE gives foreign investors greater control over important business processes, such as credit control, importation, distribution and the supply chain. It can be set up as a single entity, or, if the investor already has a trading company in a free-trade zone, can be run in parallel with the existing company.

International procurement office

For the global company sourcing from China, setting up an international procurement office can be an efficient way of taking advantage of the rising numbers of Chinese suppliers competing for international business. Procurement offices not only find but can also develop suppliers – companies such as Siemens have developed extensive supplier networks in China to service company divisions around the world. Both IBM and Hewlett-Packard have procurement offices that handle over $1.5 billion in goods each year.

Choosing a location

Location in China is a strategic choice. The criteria you use to select a location must reflect the part of the supply chain going to China, and will include government relations, proximity to suppliers and market, infrastructure, and presence or absence of other investors or competitors. If you are setting up a domestic distribution centre, you will need a different type of location to one suitable for an international distribution centre. If you are planning to produce finished products for export, your plant should be near a port, whereas finished products for local markets may need to be made in several inland locations. Services should be located as near as possible to potential customers, and consumer products need to be accessible to consumers. Ikea builds stores where there are good public transport links, makes sure there are plenty of taxi lanes so customers can take purchases home easily, and accommodates rising car ownership by creating adequate parking space as well.

> Finished products for local markets may need to be made in several inland locations

We started negotiations with a potential partner in Shanghai, but I got put off by them and instead went round the country looking at alternatives. I went to Harbin and Wuhan and found out a lot about labour rates, land use fees, and the types of deal I could get in different parts of China. Eventually the guys in Shanghai asked me to come back, and I ended up getting a much better deal because I had been out on my own and collected this information.

Bill Thompson, Clyde Blowers

You must do your due diligence on locations or the cost benefits that you expect from going to China may disappear. Shanghai is a very attractive location at first glance. It has a population of twenty million, accounts for 30 per cent of China's foreign exports and 25 per cent of all foreign direct investment into China. More than five hundred multinational companies have their regional headquarters in Shanghai, and it is also home to the world's busiest H&M clothing store. But all this comes with high property prices and high labour costs. Since labour costs were a key part of General Motors' China-specific strategy to produce cheap minivans for the local market, the company went to Luizhou instead, 1,200 miles inland, where labour costs are half that in Shanghai. In 2007 General Motors was investing $350 million in an engine plant in Luizhou.

> Clients who set up in Beijing do so either because they are in a restricted industry where they have to be near the government, or because they have a long-standing client from Beijing and feel obliged to locate near them.

> Kristina Koehler, Klako

Location factors such as infrastructure, market structure and tax policy can be more important than firm-specific or industry-specific factors in China. There are huge variations across regions, and local differences within regions. There can be very attractive incentive programmes associated with inland cities opening up to foreign companies, such as Chongqing, a thousand miles inland and with its population of thirty-one million growing by 40,000 a month. Here, infrastructure and proximity to market will be more important, as development away from the coastal cities can lag behind by several decades. There are also industrial parks devoted to industry sectors or nationalities, for instance the German industrial parks near Chongqing and Shanghai, and the Korean industrial park in Dandong.

> For us, the logistics infrastructure is very important. We look for waterways and space to expand. We also need to know the focus of the local government, whether they're selective about the industries they allow in, or whether they're embracing all kinds of foreign investment.

> Wangqiu Song, president, Stora Enso, China

Being in Chengdu is perfect for us. If you draw two diagonals across the map of China, you'll find Chengdu right in the middle. We're only a two and a half hour flight from anywhere in China apart from the very north. We have used the Chengdu office to work in Xian, Shanghai, Beijing, Guangzhou, all over the place.

And now that we are based here, a long-standing client in the UK is using us for projects in the region, so we're working outside of China as well.

Keith Linch, Robinson JZFZ

Entry to the WTO is reducing the attraction of special investment zones, as China gradually moves to create a level playing field for all enterprises operating in China, whether domestic or foreign. Tax laws are changing to reflect this, gradually bringing all taxation into line under the 'unified tax laws'. But this is China, where there is really no unified anything, so some areas, such as the central and western regions, and sectors, such as industrial research and development, will continue to offer incentives. Special investment zones retain some of their appeal because they tend to have good infrastructure and have been set up in locations that favour international trade.

Whatever location you choose, be prepared for yet more negotiations.

I had to begin negotiations on ten different sites, and keep those negotiations going, because you never knew whether you were going to be able to overcome all the hurdles. Several of them failed, even after six months or more of negotiations, because it suddenly turned out that you could not get planning permission for educational use, or you couldn't hold the land for more than five years, or someone else was interested in the same site. It's not so much of a problem if you're setting up in development zones, but we had to have a large plot in a central location.

Fraser G. White, Dulwich College Management International

Choice of location must also consider your staffing plans. If your strategy will depend on expats for some time, you need to choose a location that is attractive to them. Expatriate managers are expensive and overseas postings have a high failure rate. If you plan to localise your staff quickly, you need to locate where there is a good pool of local talent.

Location factors for Danfoss

Danfoss chose to locate a factory in Wuqing development park for several reasons. Being a big fish in a small pond meant that it was valuable to the local authorities and treated accordingly. Wuqing provided a good pool of qualified labour, and it was also only about two hours from Beijing, so that expats who wanted their children to attend international schools in the capital could commute.

A word about timing

The notion of an early mover advantage has businesses sometimes rushing in where angels fear to tread. There are plenty of stories of companies that failed to do their due diligence or tried to speed up the negotiating process and ended up in difficult situations that could have been avoided if they had not been in such a hurry. The beer wars of the 1990s provide a salutary lesson for those who think speed is of the essence.

Beer wars

> The Chinese beer market landscape is littered with corpses not only of foreign joint venture investments, but also of brands that launched and spent a lot of money and disappeared.
>
> Patric Dougan, general manager and China Business Development Director, Scottish & Newcastle Asia (S&N).

In the late 1980s, there were few foreign beers in China, and those were sold in free-trade zones, in shops only for foreigners and in the larger hotels. San Miguel of the Philippines was the first foreign company to start brewing in China in the early 1990s, but by 1996 there were about fifty joint ventures between foreign brewers and Chinese companies.

China was an attractive market, consuming roughly half of all beer drunk in Asia. Beer output was growing faster than anywhere else in the world, second only to the US, and, since per capita consumption was still low, the market appeared to have huge potential, growing by 10–25 per cent a year. Anheuser Busch invested $150 million in two joint ventures, Miller believed it had bought a 20 per cent share of the Beijing market for $100 million. Foreign companies rushed to increase capacity to cope with the expected demand.

But losses mounted rapidly. The Chinese market was fragmented, with sales localised because of the difficulties of taking products across provincial borders; the logistics of distribution were challenging; beer drinking was seasonal, dropping by half between October and June; and retail prices were low. And while foreign companies were in too much of a rush to investigate the market thoroughly, the situation was compounded by the government, which was keen to off-load loss-making, state-owned breweries.

An intense marketing war ensued, as foreign brewers tried to capture their share of the elusive market. Foreign companies spent $15 million on advertising in Beijing, Shanghai and Guangzhou alone in 1995. By the late 1990s, companies were reporting losses of millions of dollars, and had to re-evaluate and adapt their strategies if they were to stay in the market. Desperation even led some to share brewing capacity, a previously unimaginable situation.

The benefits of being first in an area or industry sector in China can include extra incentives and concessions from local governments in regions pushing for more foreign direct investment. Early movers have more time to learn about the market and build up critical relationships with government, officials, customers and suppliers. By demonstrating their trust and commitment from an early stage, these companies can be rewarded with business advantages for some time afterwards. Windows of opportunity may close, especially in industries where the number of foreign companies permitted to operate in China or in a particular region is restricted, or where the amount of inward investment is capped.

Early movers can be rewarded with business advantages for some time afterwards

Geographical areas that are just opening up to foreign companies will not be as advanced developmentally as those that have been open for some time. Infrastructure and distribution problems are just two of the issues that the early mover in this situation will have to face. The workforce will be less experienced at operating in accordance with foreign business methods and it will be harder to recruit skilled local managers from other cities.

China takeaways

▌ Companies use a number of routes to start business operations, you need to understand each one to decide which is best for your company.

▌ Location choices are critical and need considerable research because they hinge on a range of factors, from access to the attitudes of local authorities.

▌ Don't try to cut corners on business structure or location decisions. Due diligence is required.

Novozymes: the journey from agents to WFOEs

We had been selling in China since 1972, through agents, but in 1992 we decided it was time to take China seriously, so we established a sales office in Hong Kong. Then, we decided it was time for a serious investment in China, setting up production. We set up a majority joint venture with a company in Shenyang, which we chose because our set-up at the time (with sister company Novo Nordisk) meant that we needed a pharma company partner to help on the clinical trials and drug distribution side. In early 1994, we decided on a bigger investment, a larger plant and more production capacity; we wanted to upgrade to a global, strategic facility so that we could manufacture all sorts of products. To do this, we needed to bring in the latest production and micro-organism technologies, and we needed to be fully in control, so we needed to back out of the joint venture and set up a wholly foreign owned enterprise.

It was difficult because we wanted to move to Tianjin, which was more convenient logistically, and the Shenyang government did not want to lose what was going to be a very big investment. We had to use very high-level government contacts through a Chinese-speaking member of staff at the Danish embassy. The vice-premier of China at the time, Huang Ju, visited Denmark and our CEO was able to make contact with him, and that relationship helped smooth things over in Shenyang. We got the business licence for our Tianjin production plant in 1994, and we invested something like $240 million.

We didn't come to China because of the cost, it was a strategic decision. We knew that we needed production capability in this region, and we chose China. Our processes are highly automated and we don't have large numbers of employees. Unlike Motorola here, who have 6,000 employees, we only have around 250 and that includes the cleaners, the drivers, even the gardeners. So our labour costs are not a major variable for us, we're much more concerned with R&D, high-technology equipment, etc. In reality, it doesn't cost much less to set up here than it does to set up a similar plant in the US.

While we were setting up the plant, we formed another small joint venture so that we could keep selling during the three to four years it took to build and commission the plant. At that time, WFOEs weren't allowed to import products for direct distribution, but the simplest way round this was to import products and then repackage them. So we needed a small processing plant and that's why we set up the joint venture.

Then we needed a holding company to co-ordinate everything, run the HR function and open up offices in other parts of China, and we set that up as a WFOE in 1996.

Humphrey Lau, Novozymes

How do you build the teams to cope with a constantly moving picture? Now it's time to look at the people problem – the war for talent.

5 The people problem

The talent – if it's available – is being hunted by a lot of people.

Viswa Kumar, deputy trading area manager, Ikea

O
ur people are our greatest asset… Every boss you've ever listened to, every annual report you've ever read, will tell you the same thing, it's the people that make a successful business. But as Viswa Kumar of Ikea pointed out, finding the people you need in China is hard – China is the biggest battleground in the 'war for talent'.

Why is there a war for talent? Surely there are plenty of workers in China to go round? Here's one of the myths of China – just as managers might mistakenly view China as one huge market (which we'll discuss in detail in Chapter 7), so they assume that there is a vast supply of qualified people eager to work for a foreign company. While working for a foreign company is indeed the goal of many Chinese, companies setting up in China invariably report that finding staff with the right combination of skills, qualifications, experience and language is extremely difficult.

If you are a young, ambitious Chinese college graduate with five years experience, you can pick and choose.

Niels-Erik Olsen, vice-president, Danfoss, China

Recruiting and retaining the right staff anywhere is a challenge, but if we look deeper at the issues around staffing in China, even the most experienced HR professional might think twice before taking the plunge. First, there is the language problem – who is going to do the interviewing and hiring? If the responsibility is delegated to your Chinese colleagues, how can you be sure that their choices will match your expectations? If you are one of those unusual Westerners who speaks fluent Mandarin, do you have sufficient cultural understanding to read between the lines of what a candidate is saying? Can you read their body language? And once you have your employees on board, can you manage them?

As one senior manager told me: 'If you can't make the people issues work, forget it.' Let's look at these 'people issues', beginning at the first stumbling blocks for foreigners – language, culture and communication. Culture permeates everything, and as we discuss the recruiting, retaining, motivating and managing issues that are unique to China, you'll begin to understand how culture shapes company structure. Whether you're trying to meld two cultures in a joint venture or develop your own Chinese staff in a WFOE, you will have to manage in the gap between your two (or more) cultures if you don't want to have to 'forget it'.

Language, culture and communication

There is not a right answer. You meet people who say it's essential to speak Mandarin. But the other school of thought is that this is such a dynamic market, having smart, flexible, experienced managers is more important than whether or not they speak the language. And being a leader is about being distant, so from the Chinese point of view, my lack of Mandarin is not really a concern.

Kabir Nath, president, Bristol-Myers Squibb China

Mandarin is the official language, and spoken by most of the Chinese population. It is a famously difficult language to learn, with a tonal system of pronunciation that gives a word several meanings, depending purely on how it is spoken. The five basic tones can also be modified according to the context of what is being said, and plenty of travel books testify to the 'stupid' foreigner who asks for their mother-in-law to be painted blue when trying to order dinner.

Learning Chinese is said to be much easier for expatriates with a Chinese partner or spouse, but not every foreigner going to China can organise their personal lives accordingly. Classroom learning is unfortunately not so effective, so if you're serious about learning Chinese, be prepared to invest a considerable amount of time if you want to become proficient.

Any time you insult China, you are dead. Just dead.

Tom Doctoroff, chief executive, J. Walter Thomson , Greater China

Learning Mandarin will not help much if you don't at the same time make an effort to understand Chinese culture.

Stories abound of disastrous mistakes that were only understood long after the event

Stories abound of disastrous mistakes that were only understood long after the event. Cultural misunderstanding can lead to misperceptions and antagonism. The best products in the world won't sell if you and your business are regarded with contempt, so it is important to develop cultural understanding right from the start.

I was at the Danish ambassador's residence for a dinner, and at eleven o'clock, he asked us to leave. It's perfectly normal in the Danish context, but you would never say that to a Chinese guest. You can't be open and frank in that way, a lot of Chinese people would see that as rude, unsophisticated, even stupid.

Humphrey Lau, president, Novozymes, China

I could write an entire book on Chinese culture. Luckily, plenty of people already have, and I would strongly recommend reading as much as you can to get a feel for the cultural differences between your country and China. But there is much in *Uncovering China* that can only be understood in the context of Chinese culture, so here I will briefly summarise the most important concepts to bear in mind when trying to understand the actions and words of your Chinese colleagues and business associates.

Chinese culture derives significantly from the teachings of Confucius, who placed the family at the heart of society.

According to Confucius, there were five cardinal relationships – between a ruler and his subject, father and son, husband and wife, older brother and younger brother, and friend to friend. Note that relationships with strangers were not part of the Confucian social order, making them inevitably part of what sociologists call the 'out-group', rather than having a place as part of the 'in-group'. This concept of 'in' and 'out' helps us not only to understand why *guanxi* is so important, but also sheds light on the ease with which the Chinese appropriate business and financial advantages from outsiders. Everything outside the business 'family' is looked on as fair game, so taking things from outsiders doesn't raise an eyebrow.

The importance of the ruler-subject relationship can be seen in what organisational anthropologist Geert Hofstede, in his ground-breaking study on organisational culture across countries, described as 'power distance'. Hofstede used this term to define a scale where high power distance represents a culture in which orders from superiors are automatically obeyed, and low power distance signifies that orders will be questioned, or decisions arrived by consultation and consensus. Interestingly, although China is thought of as a collectivist society, one in which the good of the group supersedes the good of the individual, it has one of the highest power distance ratings of the fifty countries that Hofstede studied.

The ruler-subject relationship is characterised by those below obeying those above without question, hence workers in China prefer to be told what to do, rather than to be asked what they think they should do. Many foreign companies feel that their staff do not think ahead, failing to take initiative and take the next step. For instance, in a phone call soliciting information, they will only ask for the information specified, do not expect them to think of supplementary questions in the light of the responses they receive.

> We've had our cultural problems. It has been a learning process for us and for them. Where there are conflicts due to culture, we try to meet in the middle. Our Chinese staff respect our cultural differences and we respect theirs, and we find a way to work together.
>
> Keith Linch, chief architect, Robinson JZFZ

Another critical aspect of Chinese culture for those hoping to do business there is 'face'. The Confucian notion of the individual being defined by the group he or she belongs to makes their standing within that group of paramount importance. Every person in China has face, from the subsistence farmer to the president. Face can be described as a combination of public perception, social role and self-esteem, and, crucially, it can be given or taken away by the words and actions of others. The more individualistic Western cultures find it hard to understand how important face really is, but this part of Chinese culture cannot be overestimated – the owner of Lee Der Industrial, a Chinese manufacturer that supplied toy company Mattel, suffered a massive loss of face over the recalls of millions of sub-standard toys in summer 2007 and was reported to have committed suicide. While most cases are not so severe, it is true that if you cause someone to lose face, you may never be able to repair the relationship.

Mattel saves face

Mattel's reliance on Chinese manufacturers meant it had to do something drastic to attempt to win back confidence after the massive toy recalls in 2007, and its only option was to take the blame. 'Mattel has admitted that most of the toys recalled in recent safety scares had "design flaws" and that Chinese manufacturers were not to blame,' reported the BBC website (2007). Thomas Debrowski, executive vice-president for worldwide operations at Mattel, went to Beijing to kowtow to Li Changjiang, head of China's General Administration of Quality Supervision, Inspection and Quarantine (AQSIQ), saying: 'Mattel takes full responsibility for these recalls and apologises personally to you, the Chinese people and all of our customers who received the toys.' Debrowski was duly chastised by Li Changjiang, but nevertheless Mr Li agreed to 'help' Mattel sort its problems out, 'This shows that our co-operation is in the interests of Mattel, I really hope that Mattel can learn lessons and gain experience from these incidents.'

According to Mattel (2007) this was not so much an abject apology but a statement of fact – new design standards for toys containing small magnets were applied retrospectively and older designs could not meet the new standards, 'To the extent that the Chinese were criticised for magnet-related recalls, Mattel apologised.'

Mattel made big strides towards returning face to the Chinese, by sending a very senior representative to apologise and suffer public chastisement, thus enabling the Chinese to demonstrate their superior position. At the same time, Mattel communicated with its shareholders to highlight the fact that the recalls were the result of the company applying even more stringent quality standards than before. Mattel might have been describing what it saw as the facts, but from a Chinese perspective, it was preserving its own face to its customers and shareholders.

If face can destroy relationships, it can also build them

If face can destroy relationships, it can also build them. By giving face, you demonstrate how important someone is to your network of connections and, like the proverbial pebble in a lake, the reverberations ripple outwards in ever-widening circles of *guanxi*.

So how do you avoid causing trouble over something that can be given, taken, gained or lost, but which you don't understand? The chief executive can give face by attending a meeting, signifying how important that meeting is. You can give face by accepting invitations or requests, providing suitably expensive gifts and entertainment (but not too costly, because that may make you look insensitive to the other side's ability to reciprocate) and demonstrating sensitivity to Chinese culture. You cause loss of face if you insult someone in public, whether intentionally or not, refuse an invitation or gift (implying that the invitation or gift is not grand enough for you), or refuse a favour. You may gain face by making it clear that you are learning from your Chinese colleagues and adopting some of their methods, and by demonstrating that you are part of a network (which Westerners are more inclined to think of as name-dropping) and have status within that network (don't make the mistake of leaving your position off your business card). You lose face if you behave inappropriately – losing your temper or crying demonstrates lack of self-control and weakness.

No matter how much you read, experiencing China is the only way to really learn how these cultural phenomena affect daily and business life. Above all, you must accept that understanding Chinese culture is a long-term, continual process. Companies that send expatriate staff to China for a mere three-year posting are making a big mistake.

The final factor in this triumvirate of challenges for the foreigner is the way the Chinese communicate. Anthropologist Edward T. Hall described communication styles according to whether information was transmitted implicitly or explicitly. Implicit communication was defined by Hall as 'high context', whereby much of the meaning is in the context rather than in the message itself. Explicit communication was defined as 'low context' and the meaning is clear in the message. China, Malaysia and Japan are the highest context cultures according to Hall's rankings, with Switzerland, the Netherlands and the US among the lowest.

This contrast in communication styles can be seen in the way messages are structured. The Chinese will start with the context, 'Because…' and then lead on to the point, '…therefore…' Someone from the US will start with their point, 'I believe…'; and then support this view with '…because…' Western reports of negotiations with Chinese invariably refer to the 'time-wasting' that goes on at the start, but to the Chinese, this is vital. Coming from opposite ends of the spectrum, each side may fail to hear the most important message from their counterparts simply because it does not appear at the 'right' point in the conversation.

Adjusting and adapting to communication styles is therefore essential for negotiating. Kodak's years of negotiations before it set up its innovative deal in the late 1990s led it to learn that establishing principles first and dealing with the details afterwards was the most efficient way to proceed.

Chinese communication style reflects the importance of the group and of maintaining harmony. Putting the context first can include describing all the points of view held by the group, and marks the individual's point of view or recommendation as subordinate to the group because it comes last. The onus is on you to listen carefully and consider how you phrase your responses. As Greek philosopher Epictetus (and thousands of management, self-help and other 'gurus' since) said: 'We have two ears and one mouth so that we can listen twice as much as we speak.' Perhaps nowhere is this advice more appropriate than for Westerners in China.

> Negotiation is often a problem for Europeans. Chinese see them as very impatient, they don't let things slowly digest, follow the process. Europeans tend to negotiate as a group, but to negotiate with the Chinese, they have to select a leader, even if it's only pretend.
>
> You have to analyse the situation when negotiating, if they start to get soft, then you need to get very tough. If they need time, you have to be patient and let them go at their own speed. And most importantly, you must understand the concept of 'face'. If you make people lose face, this is very bad – but some Europeans are too worried about face and they're not effective negotiators as a result. I try to sense how far I can push someone, I might get them to the point where they almost lose face and use that as pressure to get something agreed. But you really have to know what you are doing; if you go too far, that's dangerous.
>
> Then there's the concern about being cheated. The Danes are very naive in a way, because they think that everybody is honest, so they get cheated easily. But foreigners who worry too much about being cheated end up making problems for themselves, because they create unnecessary conflict in their business relationships.
>
> Humphrey Lau, president, Novozymes

Recruitment

> Your business plan has to be matched to the speed at which you can recruit and develop staff, and attracting the right people is a huge challenge in China.
>
> Kabir Nath, BMS

The pressure on recruitment is intense. New occupations, such as supply-chain and risk management, are appearing and other, more traditional, management positions are heavily in demand, and both foreign and Chinese companies are competing fiercely for the same people. A 2005 McKinsey survey estimated that Chinese companies with global aspirations would need some 75,000 senior managers with international experience in the next ten to fifteen years, but that there were only 3,000–5,000 potential candidates.

> ## The hunt is on for 'sea turtles': overseas Chinese who understand Chinese and Western cultures

The hunt is on for 'sea turtles': overseas Chinese who understand Chinese and Western cultures, are fluent in Mandarin and a foreign language, and have some overseas work experience. In 2006, the Shanghai municipal government held job fairs in several US and Canadian cities, offering incentives packages aimed at helping the government meet its target of attracting 10,000 overseas Chinese professionals back to China every two to three years. Other Chinese cities, such as Beijing, are also working to bring people back to China.

The challenge is to find candidates with the right combination of qualifications, skills, experience and language for a particular position, and establishing those criteria is important because language can sometimes be a red herring. A common trap is to hire people whose English is good, but who don't necessarily have the appropriate skills or network.

> For jobs which are China-related, like sales or operations, I think you need Chinese staff. Language is the surface thing, but the mentality and culture are key. For jobs which are internationally related, even though they're based in China, you don't need Chinese staff and so you see a lot of expats in these positions. Over the longer term, for cost and other reasons, it will become better to have Chinese people in these positions, but right now it costs about the same because Chinese with the right experience are very hard to find and expensive to hire.
>
> Humphrey Lau, president, Novozymes

If you feel that someone isn't right, get rid of them. Don't wait until it's too late. A German client was setting up a sales office in China and hired a Chinese general manager who had spent several years in Germany, spoke German and almost seemed more German than they were. But as soon as they posted him to China, he changed. He was no longer polite towards women, he yelled at me on the phone, he offended staff at headquarters when he visited. But they were reluctant to get rid of him, he had all the contacts in China. After a year and a half, he had grown their China office to eleven people but headquarters had finally had enough. They fired everybody. They had to go back and start all over again.

Kristina Koehler, director, Klako, Shanghai

If you're looking for graduates, you can find them both within China and at overseas universities. There are, not surprisingly, advantages and disadvantages for both. Chinese graduates are cheaper to hire, there are large numbers of them – for instance, 250,000 engineering students graduate each year in China – and they are generally readily available. However, while they may be able to read and write English at an acceptable level, their speaking and understanding will be poor, and they may only want a short period of employment before going abroad for further studies. The nature of the Chinese educational system will mean that they have good theoretical but weak practical skills. A recently graduated Chinese engineer may not know how to use a spanner.

Another problem could be the residence permit, or *hukou* – all Chinese have a *hukou*, which essentially defines where they can live and work. Moving to a different city may mean that they lose their entitlements to welfare benefits, such as subsidised housing and education for their children.

Chinese who graduate from overseas universities will be familiar with foreign cultures and have greater critical thinking and practical skills, but they will be more expensive to recruit and relocate, and may have to work out long notice periods if they have already taken a job overseas.

Graduate numbers game

Graduate recruitment is a numbers game. One company received 2,170 applications from graduates of the eight top Chinese universities. Of these applicants, 513 passed a logic test and moved on to the next phase, skills and language testing. Three hundred and fourteen passed this phase, the remainder were added to the company's database as potential future candidates. Interviews focusing on behaviour and attitudes whittled the group down to seventy-six potential employees. The company offered positions to forty candidates and twenty accepted, less than 1 per cent of the original applicants.

China Business Solutions, 2007

Graduate recruitment provides a ready source of candidates, and many foreign companies in China have built relationships with the most prestigious universities to try and beat their competitors to the cream of each year's graduate crop. In more specialised fields, sponsorship of research and training programmes may be essential if graduates are to have the skills you need.

Grow your own

Novozymes has three subsidiaries and one joint venture in China. The company's regional headquarters in Beijing also houses the Novozymes Research and Development Centre, which received government approval in 2002 to provide post-doctoral training.

www.novozymes.com/en

Once you start looking for people with experience, things change. Demand for such staff is extremely high and poaching appears common, although this may often be more a case of Chinese staff changing jobs for a higher salary or better position rather than downright theft by your competitor (something which we will look at in greater depth later in this chapter).

Location will again be a factor – while you might have a bigger pool of potential recruits in Beijing because there are six hundred institutions and universities, the presence of more foreign research and development centres than anywhere else in China also means that candidates will have plenty of employers to choose from.

The pressure on finding staff makes getting the recruitment process right even more critical. Just as when recruiting in your own country, there will be criteria that define the position and the successful candidate. Don't allow the differences of working in China to cloud your judgement: if you need an engineer who has worked for several years in a particular field, then no amount of fluent English will make up for a lack of experience. Your criteria may include the skills needed for the position, length of experience, market knowledge and experience working with suppliers, but most important will be to assess the candidate's integrity and personal values for their fit with your company culture. Everyone wants to recruit people who will integrate easily into their corporate culture, but the 'noise' of cultural differences can interfere with the ability to spot a good fit. So if you find a candidate who appears to reflect your corporate culture, make sure that they are also willing to learn. Skills can be taught, but attitude is hard to change.

> ## The 'noise' of cultural differences can interfere with the ability to spot a good fit

Would I choose a bright guy or a guy who is maybe not that bright but has a very positive attitude? My experience with the second type of recruit has been good. People who have a positive attitude work hard and develop on the job. If you have to choose between the best people and the right people, go for the right people.

Manish Mehra, chief executive, Berger Paints, China

There are additional cost implications of hiring in China. Your corporate culture will stem in part from where the company was founded, and Chinese recruits at most levels will have to be exposed to the 'home' culture at some point, probably fairly early on in their career with your company. They may also need to see how things are done, particularly with regards to quality. Scottish and Newcastle brings its key technical staff from China to Europe each year. This not only brings them up to date with the latest technologies, but also helps the company to stress the quality messages that are so important, especially in an industry like brewing. And don't forget, a trip to Europe gives face and strengthens ties to the group.

Company culture at Arup

Design and consulting firm Arup believes that it takes five years for recruits to absorb their corporate culture, and a variety of means is used to pass the culture on, including on-the-job training, an in-house magazine that covers Arup worldwide, and inviting staff to represent Arup at international conferences. These last two examples match well with the Chinese desire to feel part of an important group and demonstrate their position within that group. To pick the right people, Arup spends time at interview exploring a candidate's personality through their leisure and social activities outside the workplace.

Similarly, many of Danfoss's Chinese recruits spend two years in Europe, where the engineering company hopes they will learn how to behave in a more 'European' way at work, taking the initiative, participating in group discussions and contributing in a more active way to their teams. The aim for Danfoss is to build a corporate culture that is different from and stronger than either home culture, Chinese or foreign. By creating a separate family, the company creates a set of allegiances and different social and corporate bonds.

Recruitment for many companies is also about localisation, the need to develop Chinese staff to a level where they can take over from more expensive expatriate staff. But strategic expertise is hard to find in China. State-owned businesses were almost strategy-free, with every aspect of the business subject to central control and no drive to make a profit. The Chinese culture provides people who like to take orders and feel uncomfortable questioning the decisions of those around and above them, and it is difficult to find Chinese who are capable of leading teams of foreigners. While things are starting to change with the new generation of entrepreneurial Chinese, there is still a long way to go before the pool of suitable talent comes close to matching demand. So companies have to develop their own staff, and recruit accordingly. Ikea, for example, looks for values, experience in a multinational environment and leadership potential, which for them includes strategic thinking, ability to lead people, ability to handle change, ability to be an Ikea role model and communication skills.

While we can dwell on the cultural differences at length, some companies may also have to re-examine their own cultural expectations and recruit 'outside the box', like international drinks group Scottish and Newcastle – their chief brewer in China is a Chinese woman.

Training

Education in China tends to be by rote learning and theoretical – remember how engineering graduates don't know how to use a spanner? In the training context, Chinese culture manifests itself in the way that pupils are unable to question their teacher, someone with higher status than themselves. And what we would think of as shyness, or a reluctance to put one's hand up and answer a question, translates into something more significant when we link it with the concept of face. So adapting to Western-style training, which is often founded on debate, participation, challenging assumptions and learning by doing, can be a challenge for Chinese employees. This is particularly true for older employees, who have a hard time adjusting to new ways of doing things, whereas the younger generation is often keen to learn new things.

> The type and amount of training offered is one of the tools to attract the best candidates

The type and amount of training offered is one of the tools to attract the best candidates. Arup offers its staff training towards an internationally recognised chartership, including stints in overseas offices. Danfoss runs an Asian leadership programme for its young engineers as part of the company's drive to localise management, providing training in areas that Danfoss feels the Chinese education system has neglected, such as interpersonal skills and the ability to work in teams.

Training is not cheap. B&Q expects to spend the equivalent of 15 per cent of the first year's salary on training, with employees spending their first three months shadowing other employees. Novozymes' research and development centre may be about new products, but it is also focused on selecting, training and developing people whom the company hopes will become senior managers in the future.

But once you have spent the money and time on giving your staff the analytical, interpersonal and other skills that they need to compete in a global business world, there's a new problem, as Heinz Gaugl of RHI says, 'as soon as you train someone, their market value goes up'.

Retention and motivation

Retention and motivation are inextricably linked. If you can't motivate your staff, you will not be able to retain them. How companies motivate their staff is therefore an important part of their retention strategy, and while the following discussion focuses largely on retention, it will be clear that the strategies described serve to motivate as well as to retain. Raising the cost of exit is the key to keeping staff in China, and that is not purely about salary, as you will see. Aspects of Chinese culture should be used to instil a sense of family in the workforce, coupled with pride and passion in their company, so that they see leaving as a step into the unknown.

Headhunters are everywhere, and seem to have everybody's telephone number; Chinese staff send out their CVs to test their market value; competitors will offer your best employees more than double their salary to move; and companies report staff turnover of more than 15 per cent, so retention is a headache. Remember that, as with so much else, your understanding of Chinese culture will be critical to the success of your retention strategy.

Very few people leave because of the money.

Rory McGowan, Arup, China

A 2006 survey carried out by Manpower and Right Management into employee engagement and retention in Beijing, Shanghai and Guangzhou revealed interesting discrepancies between human resources staff and employees over the reasons for leaving a job. While 70 per cent of the HR people surveyed believed that the pay and benefits package was the most significant factor in an employee changing jobs, only 15 per cent of employees agreed. The employees were more concerned with career development (68 per cent) and opportunities for advancement (43 per cent). The HR department did recognise these factors as being important, but not to the same extent, and they were wrong over pay and benefits.

Salaries do have to remain competitive, but the money is only part of the overall package. China's move towards privatisation has taken away the job security and social benefits for life, the 'iron rice bowl' that the Chinese had taken for granted, and employers are now expected to shoulder some of the burden. Benefits that include help with housing, subsidised meals and medical insurance, for instance, are common. The cultural desire to be part of a group is partly driven by the support the group will give to the individual, and a strong set of benefits show how the group, your company, looks after its own.

A company that shows strong commitment to developing its employees is demonstrating that it takes a long-term view, that the employee is going to be part of the 'family' for a long time and will be able to grow within the group. China as a whole is seeing a revival of ancestor worship, the importance of the family past and present is joined by thoughts of the family's future, and companies need to tap into this feeling.

Culture can also be seen at work in the employees' view that career development and opportunities for advancement are the most important reasons for staying in a job. Advancement, new titles and greater responsibilities, are a way in which the company can give face, and the employee can gain face in front of their colleagues and their family and friends. Employees expect to progress quickly, and must be seen to do so. This can be demonstrated by adding extra stages in the hierarchy, new titles, and additional reporting layers. Sending senior staff overseas is another way of demonstrating how much the company values them.

The shortage of Chinese staff ready for senior management positions coupled with the need to demonstrate career development opportunities creates yet another problem.

If there are no Chinese in the top positions, staff equate this with a glass ceiling

If there are no Chinese in the top positions, staff equate this not with lack of experience and skills, but with a glass ceiling above which Chinese staff cannot rise. While many foreign companies operating in China seek to localise their staff, senior positions are still largely filled by expatriates because Chinese managers are simply not yet ready to take on strategic roles. The Chinese will assume that they can only go so far before an expatriate stops them advancing – and if they see that glass ceiling as immutable, they will leave. If you cannot retain your staff, you will never be able to localise.

> The real solution is you take local Chinese, keep them in Danfoss five to ten years, send them overseas for a number of years, run them through other parts of the group and eventually bring them back into managerial positions in China.
>
> Niels-Erik Olsen, Danfoss

BP seeks raw talent

BP believes in finding raw talent, providing tailored training, and engaging employees' hearts as well as their minds.

The search process encompasses university partnerships, internships and a global MBA programme, along with search firms and external assessments. The company follows strict vetting procedures using third-party organisations to check education and other qualifications, and for some roles organises drug and alcohol tests through the police.

A dedicated programme ensures that employees get the best opportunity to develop and advance their career. All BP staff in China can apply for any BP vacancy around the world that includes a relocation package, and three-quarters of BP's vacancies are filled by internal staff through a fair and transparent process. The company believes strongly in taking specialist skills to where they are needed, providing intensive language and culture training if necessary.

The company encourages and supports participation in community programmes, charities and other voluntary work at its locations, showing its commitment to Chinese society. Employee engagement is enhanced through voluntary participation in different working groups, which does not entail changing jobs but enables employees to broaden their contribution to BP's development. An employee satisfaction survey is carried out every two years.

Graduates tend to prefer to move around within the company and see the different career paths we can offer, whereas older employees, who are perhaps married and have a child, will value the benefits package more.

Helena Shen, HR director, Global Acetyls and Aromatics unit, BP

Commitment to China and the notion of family can have their drawbacks. If the boss is seen as a father figure, then if he or she leaves other employees may leave too, as they will feel that they have lost their father's protection. Companies can build on the family concept, though, by employing their staff's relatives or partners, which will strengthen connections. While Westerners may feel that this is unacceptable, it is worth remembering that, when it comes to China, one man's nepotism is another man's retention policy.

For blue-collar workers, the family aspect is very important. Danfoss has instilled a sense of pride in its workforce by making it clear that management has confidence in its workers' abilities to match international quality requirements.

Retention and motivation tips

- Have a long-term focus – the company is another family.
- Strengthen 'family' ties by employing from the same village or group.
- Use housing loans and bonus packages to lock employees in for a certain time.
- Obtain residence permits for those who must relocate.
- Demonstrate clear opportunities for career progression.
- Hold regular appraisals so that employees know when their next step will come.

- Award visible marks of progress – titles, responsibilities, staff beneath.

- Provide as much training as possible.

- Provide international experience, such as secondment to another office.

- Have a transparent localisation strategy that will develop Chinese staff to take senior, strategic roles.

Retaining and motivating expatriates

I have come here ... to develop competence and move.

Viswa Kumar, deputy trading area manager, Ikea China

From a pragmatic point of view, expatriate managers are expensive, rarely spend long enough in China to learn how to manage the Chinese, and may have problems with trust, making them less than cost-effective. But until there is an ample supply of suitably qualified senior managers in China, you must be prepared to bear the costs of expat staff.

Brilliant executives who are being posted abroad often believe that business skill is sufficient, and dismiss learning about the history, the arts, the culture, the traditions of the country where they are now expected to perform – only to find that their brilliant business skills produce no results.

Peter Drucker (1999)

Companies always waste money when they try to save money on preparing staff to take on an overseas assignment. If you have spent millions investing in your China operation, it is pointless, and probably harmful, to try and save a few hundred on expatriation costs. Language and cultural awareness training are critical, along with someone available at the new location to help if the location is difficult. Help with tax and disposing of home country housing may also be necessary. Expats who relocate with family will need extra help, an unhappy spouse is frequently cited when an overseas assignment is terminated early.

It can be hard to motivate expats who know that their main reason for being in China is to train someone to take over their job. And while we've seen that three years is not long enough to get to know China, it is probably not reasonable to expect anyone to spend more time than that on what is essentially a handover project. But while such an assignment may sound like a dead end, you need to send high-calibre staff to China, not only because they will do a better job, but also because the Chinese will view who you send as a sign of how much headquarters respects the China operation. Expatriate assignments to China will therefore have to fit clearly into the employee's career path if they are to be a success.

Managing people

Managing people who speak a different language, communicate differently, won't give what you think of as a straight answer and are sensitive to slights that you can barely detect is a challenge.

> Managing people who are sensitive to slights that you can barely detect is a challenge

Europeans who consider themselves frank are thought of as rude, expats who won't join in the company karaoke night are clearly not interested in belonging. In both these cases, the foreigner appears unintelligent and not worthy of respect. Little wonder that they have a hard time managing in China.

Based on your knowledge of Confucius and the tradition of respect for elders, you won't be surprised to learn that Chinese companies tend to be paternalistic and that leaders are expected to be caring 'fathers', guiding and teaching their employees to the greater good of the 'family', in this case the company. Building relationship was an important part of setting up in China in the first place, and, if you're going to be *paterfamilias*, it will clearly be equally important in working directly with your employees. You will need to find a way to adapt Western practices to meet Chinese expectations, while at the same time creating an environment in which the Chinese way of working can be aligned with what your local and international customers need.

Try to meet in the middle, find a way to work together and respect each other's cultures.

Keith Linch, Robinson JZFZ

Just as a manager is expected to guide and teach, he is also expected to maintain harmony in the workplace. Disrupting harmony can cause an employee, or even the company, to lose face. Public rebuke is the most obvious way you can cause someone to lose face, but excessive praise can also be a problem, because it implies loss of face in those who are not being praised. While managers might encourage competition between individual employees in the West – employee of the month is a classic example – in China it is better to reward a group or a team for meeting a target, rather than for beating other teams. And since giving face is about demonstrating standing within the group as a whole, having a team photograph taken with the boss can be more significant than a less visible financial or other prize.

Another Chinese way to maintain harmony is to send employees out to learn, rather than bringing outside consultants into the company to train. An outsider might bring discord into the 'family', and while it may take longer for external training to produce results, it could be worth the extra investment if the alternative is disruption in the workplace.

Employee satisfaction is often cited as a prerequisite for customer satisfaction – our people are our most important assets, again. With the need to maintain harmony and give face, we can see how important cultural understanding is to managing China operations and achieving that customer satisfaction.

China takeaways

▌ Your China operation will not work if you don't get the 'people issues' right, so you must take the time to learn and try to understand the cultural differences you will face.

▌ You will have to 'manage in the gap' between cultures and some companies are creating a culture that is neither home country nor China but somewhere in between.

▌ Listen first and talk later. Westerners have much to learn about this ancient civilisation.

▌ It's a very competitive labour market, and you'll have to rely on key local personnel to select the people your operations depend upon.

▌ Retention of personnel and low turnover is achieved not by money alone, but by opening up long-term prospects for the Chinese workers in your organisation. The company becomes a second family.

▌ Expatriates are expensive both financially and in the perception that they represent a glass ceiling. Make career paths and skills and experience criteria transparent so that local staff know what they need to do to progress. That means investment in training, and the development of cross-cultural skills – by your Chinese personnel, as well.

▌ Don't underestimate the amount of senior management time which needs to be focused on these issues.

▌ On IP issues, there are knowledgeable advisors such as Rouse and Co. International, who you can turn to.

Now you're ready to start looking at the nuts and bolts of doing business in China. We'll begin at the beginning – setting up operations – before moving on to starting to sell your products.

References and bibliography

BBC (2007) 'Mattel sorry for "design flaws"', BBC News website, 21 September, http://news.bbc.co.uk/1/hi/business/7006599.stm

China Business Solutions (2007) www.chinabusinesssolutions.com

Drucker, P. (1999) *Management Challenges for the 21st Century*, Butterworth-Heinemann, Oxford

Mattel (2007) media statement, 21 September, http://www.shareholder.com/mattel/downloads/09-21-07 per cent20China per cent20Meeting per cent20media per cent20Statement.pdf

Climbing the ladder in the right order: setting up operations

> You have to climb the ladder in the right order. Focus first on quality and delivery; once these are secure, focus on cost and engineering issues; and, only later, deal with knowledge transfer and R&D.
>
> Kjeld Staerk, Danfoss

You cannot do everything at once when starting up in China. While cost leadership is critical to your competitive advantage and China looks like the answer, the all-too-frequent headlines about product recalls suggest that 'made in China' can be an expensive proposition if you do not get it right. Try to rush things in China and you may lose any cost advantages you were expecting to gain.

That Danfoss quote was right on two counts: there is a ladder to climb; and you can't miss out any of the steps. Only when you're established on each rung should you look at moving up to the next. Given the likelihood of China setting the world price as a platform for global manufacturing for years to come, it's worth taking a very close look at that ladder and what you'll need to consider if you're to reach the top. But remember that everything else in this book must be taken into account as you set up operations in China, otherwise you might climb the ladder only to find that it is leaning on the wrong wall.

Quality: the supplier problem

> We were worried about quality in China. Since our production is not much cheaper here anyway, our worries about quality may

have led us to spend too much on establishing production. We did think about a two-tier production strategy, with a very lean operation producing cheaper products, but our fear of compromising on quality steered us away from that.

Humphrey Lau, president, Novozymes, China

Quality is the biggest headache for companies sourcing and producing in China. Writing in the *Financial Times* in 2007, Arthur Kroeber, managing editor of the *China Economic Quarterly*, described the preceding week as one of 'carnage', in which recalls were announced for eighteen million toys (Mattel, US), vinyl baby bibs (Toys 'R Us, US), mattresses (Netherlands), fruit and vegetables (Thailand) and a home diabetes test kit (US), all made or produced in China, and all feared contaminated with dangerous chemicals.

More seriously, quality problems kill people. Numbers in China are always difficult to confirm, but both adults and babies have died as a result of contaminated or fake drugs and foodstuffs. In 2007,

The former head of the Chinese State Food and Drug Administration was executed for corruption

the former head of the Chinese State Food and Drug Administration (SFDA), Zheng Xiaoyu, was executed for corruption and the 170,000 medical licences granted during his tenure were put under review. Jane Macartney (a descendant of Lord George Macartney, the eighteenth-century British envoy who famously refused to kowtow to the Emperor) of *The Times* listed at least four deaths and 50,000 babies hospitalised because of contaminated baby formula in 2008. The SFDA, which was created in 2003 to consolidate food regulations and enforce the 1993 Product Quality Law, is clearly a long way from delivering on the promises it made to crack down on companies that do not comply with quality stipulations in the wake of Zheng's execution. The problem is systemic and China is yet to demonstrate that making an example of some of those involved makes any more difference than generating a few headlines.

It's no surprise, therefore, that everyone I spoke to about setting up operations in China stressed that quality is the first thing to get right. But the problem is not just about the products themselves. The increasing scrutiny of all things Chinese by journalists, analysts, human rights activists and other commentators puts not only how good your products are but how they are made in the spotlight. If your supplier produces perfect products, but the workers who make them live in poor conditions and work long hours, your brand will suffer just as much as if it was attached to a shoddy product. However, all this does not put companies off – in 2003, Wal-Mart purchased $15 billion in goods from Chinese suppliers and General Motors spent $200 million on car parts made in China.

Wal-Mart expects...

Wal-Mart's sustainability summit held in Beijing in October 2008 was an emphatic demonstration of what it expected from China, and was attended by nearly 1,000 suppliers, Chinese officials and representatives of other organisations. Lee Scott, Wal-Mart's chief executive and president, told the audience: *'I firmly believe that a company that cheats on overtime and on the age of its labour, that dumps its scraps and its chemicals in our rivers, that does not pay its taxes or honour its contracts – will ultimately cheat on the quality of its products.'*

Stricter requirements for suppliers to meet environmental laws and regulations were announced, along with expectations for greater transparency, including the names and locations of all sub-contractors. Mike Duke, vice-chairman of Wal-Mart Stores, stated that compliance would be monitored in a number of ways, including random inspections. The supplier agreements were to be phased in starting from January 2009 in China, and then rolled out around the world by 2011.

Solving the supplier problem is 'a pain in the butt'...

Ninety per cent of our raw materials come from Chinese suppliers. We have quality management systems and operating procedures to ensure that everything is up to global standards, we also incorporate sustainability, environmental and social criteria. Our local auditors apply global standards, they travel to all our suppliers to check them, and report back to the CEO and the chairman of the board of directors. There is no way of getting round our standards, and we're very proud of them, we even brag about them. But frankly, it's a pain in the butt. It is very time-consuming and adds significant costs to meet these standards. For instance, we might find we have suppliers very far away, because we can't find one nearer who is willing to install the necessary waste water treatment facilities, or they don't pay medical insurance for their workers, or there is something else that they won't comply with. But we can't change our global rules just to accommodate China, we have to find suppliers that are willing to meet our requirements – and be audited to ensure that they are complying.

Humphrey Lau, Novozymes

While the situation in China is improving as international experience mounts, for many companies, getting quality still means choosing the best supplier you can find and then investing in training and development to achieve the quality levels required. Volkswagen spent ten years, from 1986 to 1996, building up the supply chain to service its plant in Shanghai and Ikea has a compliance manager and six full-time auditors working with its suppliers across China.

Iway – the Ikea way

Iway specifies what Ikea expects of its suppliers worldwide. An evaluation checklist for potential suppliers covers eight 'must-haves', including business licences, and compliance with laws regulating environmental pollution, safety standards and working conditions. Having passed the eight 'must-haves' and been evaluated for quality and production set-up, the potential supplier goes through an audit with the Ikea compliance team. An action plan is generated to indicate where improvements must be made, and these are followed up by the purchasing teams.

Like Ikea, Novozymes and many others, you need a checklist for what you expect from your suppliers, which you must discuss with them and audit regularly. You need to explore everything from basic skills to management competencies and financial soundness, along with willingness to learn and awareness of intellectual property (IP) rights.

Choosing a supplier

Always check references against your selection criteria, and try to get references not only from other clients, but also from purchasing agents or other intermediaries who have dealt with your potential supplier.

▌ Do they understand the levels of quality and service you require?

- Look at other products and operating procedures.

- Ask yourself if you feel a good working relationship can be established so that any misunderstandings and problems can be sorted out easily.

▌ Do they have the ability and equipment to produce what you want?

- Check equipment, prototypes and samples.

- Check the skills of employees, particularly in critical positions.

▌ Do they have the capacity to deliver the quantities you need on time?

- Have they delivered this quantity before?

▌ Do they have the flexibility and reliability you need?

- Assess management skills.

- Check financial soundness.

- Check location and access (including risk of natural disasters such as floods preventing shipment).

▌ Do the costs add up?

- Include shipping time and costs, training, technical support, travel and other costs for expatriate staff.

▌ Do you trust them with the necessary level of intellectual property (IP)?

- Check their understanding of business ethics.

- Explore local interpretation of IP laws and level of enforcement.

▌ Do they respect international labour laws?

  – Check how they treat their employees and sub-contractors.

  – Make sure they do not use child labour.

Adapted from *Behind the Kaleidoscope: A Guide to China Entry and Operations*, p.440)

In working with suppliers, you will be attempting to match international consumer expectations with how your suppliers treat their employees, and hence indirectly the Chinese employees' needs themselves, something that at times seems almost impossible. For instance, while Westerners express their horror at employees working twelve hours a day, seven days a week in a 'sweatshop', the employees are probably living in a workers' dormitory, far from home and only there to make money for their family. A mental shift is required if we are to reconcile our own desires with those of the people making our toys and T-shirts.

> People in the West should not adopt the culturally imperialistic notion that everyone shares their emotions

People in the West should not adopt the culturally imperialistic notion that everyone shares their emotions – particularly when the price we pay for that T-shirt is considerably more than a month's wages to the person that made it.

> One of the challenges of working with Chinese suppliers is compliance with working hours. If we insist that a supplier enforces working hours regulations, then his employees will leave to go and earn more money at another company, one that lets them work longer hours. Migrant workers who are only interested in sending as much money as possible back to their family have little time for concepts such as work-life balance.

> Viswa Kumar, deputy trading area manager, Ikea

Companies can use their reputation and purchasing clout to encourage change in their suppliers. Here is Ikea's Kumar again:

> Probably most suppliers in China don't have accident insurance for their workers. We insist on it, if they want to work with Ikea.

We also insist on certain space and hygiene standards in workers' dormitories, and don't work with suppliers who charge a deposit for uniform and tools. Suppliers often complain that migrant workers are likely to leave without warning, taking their tools with them, and that's why deposits are necessary. But to us, it smacks of bonded labour. Suppliers will comply with our requirements because we want long-term relationships, ten to fifteen years, we don't just buy and run. And working with Ikea is like a certification, they will win business from other retailers because they work with us and our reputation is known.

Viswa Kumar, deputy trading area manager, Ikea

Employment laws that came into force on 1 January 2008 may go some way towards assuaging the concerns of foreign consumers. New contracts, specified rights and a clear recognition of the lawful rights and interests of employees (as well as employers) all stem from WTO accession and China's need to meet Western expectations. But laws are only as good as their enforcement, and, just as with intellectual property and other trade rules in China, there is still a way to go before such laws are uniformly applied.

Another part of the supplier equation stems from the cultural side discussed previously. Western companies used to a two-way dialogue where the suppliers contribute their own experience to refining specifications are in for a surprise. Chinese suppliers expect instructions: 'Here are the specifications, get on with it.' On the plus side, good suppliers tend to be flexible and quick to learn processes and systems.

We work hard to build relationships with our suppliers. We produce written information to explain what we expect from them, they have formal, in-house training with our team, and a team of international inspectors then follows up. If, once they understand what we want to do, they sign on the dotted line, then it's the start of an ongoing programme of development. It's not just about finding a supplier with the right price and walking away saying 'job done'. It's long term and building people up takes time. Many of our most successful suppliers have been with us since we started here seven years ago. They have come on the journey with us.

Mark Ladham, B&Q

While trust and a long-term orientation are as important as always in China, the supplier relationship is one area where *guanxi* does not hold sway over other considerations, such as price and product competition. Increasing international experience has also begun to shift the power in supplier relationships – good, reliable suppliers are in demand and can turn a potential client down if they consider the order volume unattractive. Other factors, such as the face gained supplying a particular international brand, may also come into play.

But where price is the only driver of the supplier relationship, 'quality fade' can be an issue. The quality of the first few shipments may be very high, but as corners and costs start to be cut, the quality of shipments can deteriorate. Technical requirements must be clearly stated, in writing, and suppliers must understand that unsatisfactory goods will be rejected. Batches can be checked by one of your own engineers or technical experts on site, or via an independent inspection company. The physical or chemical properties of raw materials also need to be checked, because using poor quality raw materials will have ramifications on the production line.

> All of a sudden the quality of castings we were getting from one of our suppliers started to fall off, even though they had all the inspection equipment for testing metal samples and the finished products. It was obviously a process problem, somebody was not paying enough attention to their job. So we brought in a quality manager from the UK and a specialist from a casting association in the UK, and these two guys spent a few days at the factory, going back through the whole casting process right to the beginning. They documented everything and checked all the inspection points, made sure the operators were getting all the necessary training, did everything they could to make sure the quality process was embedded. It seems to have worked.
>
> Bill Thompson, chief executive, InBulk Technologies, and director Clyde Blowers

If there are quality problems, the issue may be resolved through discussions with the supplier, particularly if you are establishing a relationship founded on potential long-term benefits to both sides.

If the problems are more systemic, then there is a choice between investing in the supplier to improve things or finding another source. If a supplier needs infrastructure improvements, sometimes it is simply too expensive to bring them up to scratch.

United Nations guidelines

Some companies, such as Danish mechanical and electronic engineering conglomerate the Danfoss Group, supply themselves – Danfoss China's biggest non-Chinese supplier is other factories within the group. But the same quality requirements apply to all suppliers. Danfoss treats all suppliers equally, whether they are in China, Europe or the US, and whether they are part of the group or not. The company has a code of conduct based on United Nations guidelines regarding the treatment of workers, use of child labour and corruption, and uses this to audit suppliers. Where there are quality issues, the company decides whether continuing the relationship with that supplier is viable, and invests time and money improving the supplier if the answer is yes.

Standards

If it is commercially necessary to apply internationally recognised standards as well as your own criteria, there are plenty to choose from. BSI British Standards points out that 'There are literally thousands of certification marks available,' including the 27,000 it has in its standards library, ranging from internationally recognised specifications to company manuals. Along with regulatory standards, there are also industry standards. A car made in China may pass the minimum mandated European safety criteria, but may not be competitive because consumers require their car manufacturers to 'go the extra mile' and demonstrate enhanced safety features.

The most obvious and relevant standard for China-based operations aimed at global markets is ISO 9000, which deals with quality management systems, although ISO 14000, which is concerned with environmental management systems, is rapidly assuming equal significance, and it would seem logical to adopt both in China operations. However, ISO standards are expensive and time-consuming to implement. If you decide that you need to adopt one of the ISO 9000 standards, for instance, you will have to develop quality management systems by identifying best practice, define the systems and processes and then train staff and managers to meet the requirements. This is not an undertaking for the faint-hearted, an ISO standard can be several hundred pages long and the level of detail very high, so you have to begin by defining and allocating the tasks involved. Once systems that meet ISO standards have been devised and implemented, internal auditing must be carried out before accredited external ISO auditors are called in.

Not surprisingly, the challenges to getting ISO accreditation in China are more complex than simply deciding who does what.

> The challenges to getting ISO accreditation in China are more complex than simply deciding who does what

Companies report institutional resistance to the amount of documentation and training needed, stemming from an attitude that quantity is better than quality. There is a risk that companies will do the minimum to pass accreditation, and then revert to old, more familiar ways. And since implementation of ISO standards is relatively new in China, there is a shortage of local, qualified ISO assessors. Foreign buyers sometimes insist that an ISO audit is carried out by a specific auditor from overseas rather than rely on the often newly qualified local auditors, and this adds to the time and expense of accreditation.

Does the cost of achieving ISO standards outweigh the benefits? If you're aiming for the Chinese domestic market, it might be tempting to do without, but it is important to look ahead. The pace of change in China is such that the domestic market will increasingly come to look like other markets, and standards will be as important to local sales as they are to international sales. Start-up companies hoping for a market listing somewhere down the line are recommended to behave like public companies from as early as possible, and the same logic applies to companies setting up in China when it comes to standards. What sort of behaviour will benefit your company ten years from now?

It can be done – within two years of starting operations in China, two Swiss engineering companies believe they have better batch consistency and scrap rates from China than from the home operations. As with so many things in China, it's about time, patience, understanding and commitment.

> Many of our breweries here are as good as our breweries in Europe. Some in the West aren't so good, but there's a genuine commitment to improving quality across the business.
>
> Patric Dougan, general manager, Scottish & Newcastle, China

Delivery

> We had a few disasters at the beginning, but you have to keep working things out. For instance, we had some quality problems at our factory in Shanghai. They were manufacturing gearboxes, and they knew exactly what they were supposed to do for quality checks, but there was also a target for delivery. It seemed like you could have a quality target or a delivery target, but not both. You have to have determination and patience, and remember that it's all about relationships.
>
> Bill Thompson, Clyde Blowers

A 2002 Michigan University survey of retail buyers in China revealed that quality was the most important criteria in selecting a supplier, but that a problem with suppliers once quality had been dealt with was delivery of the goods themselves. A Swiss China survey published in 2006 stated that 'suppliers rarely deliver properly on [the] first order'. Delivery problems referred to included varying purity of chemicals (and not just lower, some were delivered at a higher purity than required, which was assumed by the supplier to be 'better'), incorrect labelling, incomplete or wrong packaging, incorrect packing lists, substitution of one material for another, and a drop in quality to meet delivery deadlines.

Delivery logistics in China are fragmented and subject to local variations in regulations and certifications as well as national requirements. Consumer products in particular may require health and sanitation certificates depending on their place of origin and destination. Customs clearance specifications for moving goods in and out of provinces vary, and local governments can introduce rules at will. You will probably have to develop your local supply chain, and learning the rules and regulations for each region and province you operate in or ship to will be time-consuming and expensive.

Wal-Mart has split its supply chain into suppliers that supply all its stores in China, and others who only supply locally. The company has a nationwide supply chain with two centralisation points, one at Shenzhen in the south and one at Tianjin in the north. Suppliers who sell to Wal-Mart nationwide use these distribution centres, those who sell locally tend to deliver direct to the stores. Smaller companies don't have the benefit of such a large organisation behind them, and have to rely on other operators. Large sums of money are being invested in China by foreign-owned freight and delivery companies. FedEx has been operating in China since the 1980s, set up an Asia-Pacific hub in Guangzhou in 2005, and has a next-business-day domestic express service serving two hundred cities throughout China. In 2003, DHL began a $200 million, five-year investment programme in China to expand its range of services.

Delivery can also be a victim of geography. If your supplier is located far from major infrastructure, difficult terrain and natural disasters can interfere. The perfect supplier may not be so perfect if they are in the mountains, or in the middle of a flood plain.

> The perfect supplier may not be so perfect if they are in the mountains, or in the middle of a flood plain

Costs

When we started sourcing in China, the benchmark was to find a product that would end up having a price in store in Europe that was comparable to if the product was made in Europe – so the purchase price, the logistic cost, the shipping cost, everything to get that product to the stores had to be included.

Viswa Kumar, deputy trading area manager, Ikea

It is difficult to estimate savings associated with sourcing in China because of additional costs. Unit labour costs can be just one-thirtieth of those in Europe or the US, but total operational cost has many components. There are cost effects in process and supply chain inefficiency, the need to audit suppliers regularly to ensure that system, process, quality and regulatory requirements are met, and the possible damage to the brand if poor quality products are shipped.

Despite the apparent low cost of labour, the biggest cost mentioned is people – as pointed out in the previous chapter, salaries and other benefits are rising as supply shrinks below demand, not only for experienced workers but also the less skilled. There is no longer an inexhaustible supply of workers, and for companies recruiting for jobs typically carried out by women, populations skewed by the one-child policy add to the challenge. Another people cost is training, which is not only becoming ever more important as international and domestic customers become more demanding, but also becoming a bigger factor in overall costs. Efficiency improvements are critical when price is being squeezed from all directions.

The cost of inefficiency is very hard to manage. You see that everywhere, but in China it is a big problem. The Chinese work long hours, but the way they work is not always efficient. Improving efficiency by just 50 per cent makes an enormous difference.

Humphrey Lau, Novozymes

The cost of deliveries is an issue in China, even for goods that will be sold in the domestic market rather than exported elsewhere. Logistics in China accounts for a fifth of GDP, compared with about 8 per cent in the US. Half as many companies in China outsource their logistics than in the European Union, so there is a considerable amount of duplication and under-utilisation in the transportation sector, leading to a cumbersome and inefficient system.

Despite China apparently adding the equivalent of three to four 500 megawatt power plants to the national power system every week, some areas still have to cope with regular power cuts, and compensating for this by installing generators adds another cost. At the same time, as energy production bows to demands to meet international environmental standards, it becomes more expensive.

Not all costs are directly associated with your operations in China. Any negative connotations associated with being 'made in China' have to be countered. For business-to-business (B2B) companies, that often means flying customers to China to see for themselves the efforts you put into the quality and reliability of your products.

Engineering

While the Western trend is towards automation, labour-intensive production in China may actually be the cheaper option, and this will have to be factored into production operation decisions. But the days of being able to dismantle outdated plant in Europe and take it to China to set up an old-style production line are over. China's own plant manufacturing industry has rushed to meet the demands of businesses and consumers, and pollution and other controls are much more stringent.

In the past, the government promoted the use of Chinese-built machinery by charging very high import duty on foreign equipment when an equivalent was available from Chinese manufacturers. Conversely, equipment that was not available in China had much lower import duties, as part of the government's efforts to attract new technology. One company pointed out that, while 90 per cent of the machinery in its plant was Chinese-made, it only accounted for 66 per cent of total equipment costs.

WTO accession has, in theory, created a level playing field as far as production plant is concerned, but the picture is still not clear.

WTO accession has, in theory, created a level playing field as far as production plant is concerned

In September 2008, news agency Xinhua reported that import tariffs on spare parts for large machinery, such as transformers and coal refinery equipment, were being cut, but that tax exemptions on complete machines were being removed. Locally manufactured plant still tends to be of lower quality and have a shorter lifetime, and it is still complicated to balance this against the variable costs of importing similar equipment from overseas.

Knowledge transfer

As is clear from the above discussions on quality, delivery and costs, the China operation inevitably comes with a considerable knowledge transfer burden, in terms of both processes and technology. You will have to educate your JV partner or subsidiary, or the staff in your WFOE, to do things your way, to conform to the systems and processes that will help your China operation meld with other operations in the home country and elsewhere, while at the same time adapting your knowledge and systems to make them 'China-friendly'. You will also have to address the fact that, despite signing up to protect IP rights when it joined the WTO, in China infringements abound and regulatory enforcement is weak. We'll look at IP in more detail shortly, but we'll start with the questions you must ask about your products and your China operations.

If you are planning a JV, are you willing to transfer knowledge to your Chinese partner? The decision rests on how important the Chinese partner is and the ownership structure. There is a risk that your partner may use the knowledge gained from you in other contracts with other partners, and there is also a risk of losing proprietary technologies once transferred. Trust is critical, and the risks associated with sharing valuable information mean that often only mature technologies are transferred. As well as possibly unquantifiable risks, there are also costs involved when driving knowledge transfer across borders, and these too will affect your willingness to go ahead.

Can you transfer sufficient knowledge effectively? Think about your original knowledge base and the competencies of those who must pass this knowledge on. They will almost inevitably be expats sent to China for this purpose only. Will they accept that their aim is to work themselves out of a job? Do they have sufficient soft skills, such as language, interpersonal contact and coaching skills? If you're starting a WFOE, you can ensure that training budgets are spent on just that, but a JV partner might find other uses for the money.

Is there a capacity to learn? There may well be an emphasis on training, but you will need to determine how successfully that training is put into action. How qualified are the employees to gain and use the knowledge? Location will come into this, because big cities and high-tech areas often draw better qualified staff. However, companies often find staff are better at acquiring technologies than managerial skills. Technology knowledge does not have cultural overtones, it does not need to be 'translated' for application in the Chinese context. In addition, Marxist ideology maintains that technological expertise is the primary stimulus for economic, institutional and cultural change, and in the past state-owned enterprises have emphasised technology know-how over management know-how. Management skills, on the other hand, have a cultural context that makes them much more difficult to transfer. Management in China can be seen as a collection of number- and target-driven techniques rather than as a way of thinking and acting.

Is there willingness to learn? Employees are often incentivised by a link between performance and reward, but you may need to establish an equivalent link between learning and reward. Younger, better-educated Chinese staff are more keen to learn new skills, whereas older staff prefer more overtime work to learning. Again this is the old SOE mentality and it could form a barrier to knowledge transfer.

Intellectual property

I have great confidence that over the course of time China will be a marketplace that increasingly respects intellectual property – because innovation is one of the key themes of this present government and to have an innovative environment you have to be able to encourage people to develop their own intellectual property.

Scott Kronick, China president, Ogilvy

The point about IP in China is that the party-state could stop all the problems tomorrow. But it doesn't. This suggests that it is not policy to stop IP theft in China. Hence the difficulty in protecting IP, in enforcing regulations and in seeking redress when IP rights have been infringed. With that in mind, let's take a look at the problem and what some companies are doing about it.

The China Anti-Counterfeiting Coalition (CACC) in 1999 reported that 15–20 per cent of products sold under CACC-member trade names were fakes, and that the problem of fakes in second- and third-tier cities was much higher, at 80–100 per cent. Chinese government estimates suggest that $19–24 billion in counterfeit goods were sold on the domestic market in 2001, and some commentators believe that this figure is an underestimate. In written testimony to the US Senate in 2006, Professor Daniel C. K. Chow stated that 'Microsoft's annual losses alone due to commercial piracy in China are estimated to be £10 billion.'

> ## Of greater concern to a company setting up in China is that the counterfeiters are getting better

Chow also pointed out that, 'Despite the intense international attention focused on the counterfeiting problem in China for the past decade, counterfeiting in China appears to be getting worse, not better.' The US customs service reported seizing counterfeit and pirated products from China valued at over $87 million in 2004. But while the sheer volume of counterfeit products sold in and outside China is alarming, perhaps of greater concern to a company setting up in China is that the counterfeiters are getting better at what they do.

> When you go back ten to fifteen years, it was quite obvious which was the real thing. Today... we have to send it back to the engineers in Europe... and they take it apart and analyse it before they can find out whether it comes from a Danfoss factory or somewhere else.
>
> Niels-Erik Olsen, Danfoss

So how do you protect IP? The first thing is to decide what has to be taken to China and what should stay at home. Understand that licensing your technology to a Chinese firm is equivalent to selling it by instalments, because at the end of the agreement regulations ensure that the local firm keeps the technology.

> A huge state-owned distillery approached us to set up a joint venture, but the distance between us was too large. For four years, they bought our [bottle] caps, then they decided to make their own. This didn't work. Although the caps look simple, there's a lot of high technology in the mould, assembly and decoration processes, and their caps didn't work. So they came back to us and reopened negotiations. Eventually, we reached a joint venture agreement where we would sell them one production line for one specific product, train their technicians in Italy and help them set up production. We expected that, after starting with one line, eventually we would supply all their packaging needs. But after a year of providing technical assistance, they shut the door in our face. They started making modifications, decided to make their own moulds, and now I think they have the biggest factory in the world for moulds. We just get the royalties for the original cap, it's a curious kind of licensing agreement. Lucky for us that they're honest and at least continue paying the royalty.

> Enrico Perlo, president, Guala Closures, China

Intellectual property strategies for foreign companies in China focus on staying ahead of counterfeiters as well as competitors. Tactics to achieve this tend to polarise around two methods. One is to keep China operations one step behind technologically, so that counterfeiters will not be able to incorporate the latest innovations. Another method is to adapt processes to make counterfeiting as difficult as possible. Danfoss incorporates its logo into moulds so that the logo is part of the product, which they point out is more difficult for counterfeiters to copy than simply sticking on a fake label. More unusual is computer software that destroys itself after it has been used to guide tools cutting unique panels for boats.

> One company has a special electro-plating technique. They produce the chemicals in Europe and then import them to do the

plating here in China, so none of the staff here know the formula for the chemicals.

Kristina Koehler, Klako

Above all, you must start by notifying what constitutes your IP, so what you're protecting is clearly defined to all parties. Explain what should be considered 'trade secrets' to JV partners and employees, and have confidentiality and non-disclosure agreements in place. Don't take the attitude that registrations aren't worth the paper they're written on, register everything you can. 'Some companies complain they're being copied but haven't even bothered to register their IP,' says Bill Thompson of Clyde Blowers.

Until a few years ago, nobody filed patents here because it wasn't worth it. About six or seven years ago, we started filing patents, and now we have a big patent operation here. The biggest fear of course is that one of our employees may leave and take some of our IP with them. We do see some of our products being copied, but they're fakes, there's none of our IP there, they are cheap, poor-quality enzymes or just a fake label. Companies that copy us are very small and disappear as soon as we try to investigate them, but they're big enough to irritate us for a while.

Humphrey Lau, Novozymes

Patents are the first port of call for technologies, but it can take up to four years to complete registration in China, by which time many companies claim that their products have already been copied and patents registered by Chinese competitors. Italian company Guala Closures ensures that it begins the registration process at the same time as it files a new patent in Italy, so that by the time the product or process reaches China, its patents should be protected. Guala Closures also registers many 'utility models' in China, a lower level of protection than a patent but under which disputes are also settled at a lower judicial level, which can be quicker.

However, IP is not just about patents. A bigger issue in China are trademarks and copyright. The vast majority of the computer software and DVDs for sale in China are thought to be counterfeit.

Recent editions of programs such as Adobe Photoshop are available for less than a dollar, and the latest US cinema releases are often for sale on Chinese streets within days.

Your company name is precious. Construction hoardings can carry the name of foreign companies even when those companies have had nothing to do with the project, the prestige of the foreign name giving the project greater 'face'. One British company, realising this, registered their name in China before signing their first JV agreement, and made sure to register variations because the Chinese character system means that there are often several ways of writing the same thing. Another company reports having their brochure copied by competitors so that when they presented their own to potential clients, they also had to convince the client that they were the real thing. US chain Starbucks spent two years fighting a local coffee chain for trademark violations, eventually winning in 2006. The case hinged on the dates when Starbucks and its competitor had registered their very similar names.

So what do you do when you find a problem? China's action plan on IPR Protection 2007 cites two hundred and seventy-six measures that were being pursued in efforts to address the counterfeiting problem. The Chinese legal framework for IP is compliant with a number of international agreements, and civil litigation via the People's Court is becoming more common. The relevant government body, the Intellectual Property Office for patents, the State Administration of Industry and Commerce for trademarks, and the National Copyright Administration for copyrights, can also be asked to act, and this route is sometimes cheaper and quicker, although disputed rulings will end up in court anyway. Specialist IP panels have been set up to advise the Intermediate People's Courts where IP cases are usually heard, and can be found in major cities, provinces and special economic zones. IP rights can also be recorded with customs, to take advantage of laws regarding the seizure of suspected counterfeit goods, and the chance that the infringement can be dealt with via customs rather than going through more expensive and time-consuming court proceedings.

One problem is that fakes are being put on sale by distributors without logos, then when the customer comes to pick the product up, the distributor adds a logo sticker. So if we go and raid them, officially there aren't any fakes because there aren't any logos on the products.

Niels-Erik Olsen, Danfoss

Enforcing IP law is still viewed as difficult, and perhaps impossible in areas where the local economy is driven by the production of counterfeit goods and vested interests hold sway. Obtaining damages awarded in court may be more trouble than it is worth, and often foreign companies regard litigation more as a means of sending a message to would-be counterfeiters than as a source of reparation. While many companies, like Starbucks, recommend going the official route, citing that this demonstrates how seriously the infringement is taken, some have come up with more creative solutions, finding uniquely 'Chinese' ways of addressing the problem.

Obtaining damages awarded in court may be more trouble than it is worth

We hired a detective to help us, we collected a lot of information and engaged a PR company in China. When we finally felt that we had enough information, we went to the authorities and presented it. They raided the company and now the president is in jail. Then we had the PR company produce an article about this in which we praised the local authorities... so the authorities were happy because they felt they had done a good job and we recognised it. And companies that read the article could see that we were serious about catching fakes, so if they wanted to copy, they'd be better off copying somebody else.

Jorgen Mads Clausen, chief executive, Danfoss

Another situation highlighted by Danfoss demonstrates the need for co-operation with competitors suffering the same problem.

We see factories where they produce not only Danfoss fakes, but [also] Emerson fakes, AB&B fakes and Siemens fakes.

Niels-Erik Olsen, Danfoss

Enforcement is expected to become stronger because the government is focused on what is good for Chinese companies. As local firms start to suffer from the counterfeiters as much as foreign firms, and as Chinese companies start to compete internationally, they will have their own IP to protect and will look to the government for help. In the meantime, take every precaution and choose your battles wisely.

Minimising IP risk

▌ Think carefully about what level of IP you include in your China operation, yesterday's or tomorrow's.

▌ Make it difficult for counterfeiters to copy what you do.

▌ Define your IP clearly: register everything (technology, patents, trademarks, copyrights); define trade secrets in writing; have confidentiality and non-disclosure agreements in place.

▌ Decide how you will tackle any infringements.

▌ Take steps to reduce risk, such as reducing staff turnover and restricting sensitive information to those who need it.

IP in their heads

One Australian ship-building company operating in China believes that it is safe from IP theft because of the nature of its business. Each ship it builds is highly customised, and while counterfeiters might be able to copy the standard plans, without the background knowledge and understanding behind those plans they will not be able to customise to each particular client's specifications. The Australians believe that the IP in their heads is worth more than the IP on paper. This approach would not work for everybody, but for the Australians the nature of the sector combined with their tacit knowledge, entrepreneurial approach and constant innovation, keep them ahead of the game. That's the theory, anyway.

Research and development

By the end of 2007, the Ministry of Commerce had registered 1,160 research institutions set up in China by multinational corporations.

In just one month, October 2008, Nestlé announced a $10.2 million R&D centre in Beijing; IBM opened a new R&D lab in Shanghai and opened an extension to the IBM China Research Laboratory in Beijing, and pharmaceutical group Sanofi-Aventis announced it was expanding its R&D facility in Shanghai, launching a new biometrics centre in Beijing and entering a partnership agreement with the Shanghai Institutes for Biological Sciences to work on novel drugs. The move by Sanofi-Aventis' located the complete drug development pipeline, from discovery to final clinical trials, in China.

Historically, companies set up R&D in China only for product development and localisation, because IP problems were too great a barrier to putting any basic research in the country. Yet, product development in China is essential for companies wishing to sell locally and reduce costs. In 2003, running an R&D centre in China was a tenth of the cost of running a similar centre in the US, although prices have risen, and such investments are popular.

Chinese researchers tend to be very good at development research. The government has ramped up the provision, and take-up, of postgraduate education, and also acted to encourage those who studied overseas to return to China. But the education system does not encourage innovation, and finding staff with initiative and a creative mindset is not easy.

Another advantage of basing product development for China in China is speed, no bad thing in a rapidly changing market.

> Our main research is done in Europe, but we have a research team in China for speed reasons. If you're going to improve or modify your product and have to make a lot of small trials, if you always ship them to Europe and wait until the results come back, you're too slow.
>
> Gerald Kaufmann, general manager, Liaoning RHI Jinding Magnesia

Basing R&D in China also brings other benefits, with a laboratory or research institute being a good tool for building networks, expanding *guanxi* and forming strategic partnerships.

Research centres are typically associated with a university, which by default gives them good ties to government and thus better chances of access to state procurement offices. Companies in highly regulated sectors, such as Alcatel in telecoms, use their research bases in China to ensure that they are well placed to work with the government on industry standards and technology choices.

Continuing efforts to meet WTO requirements and establish legal enforcement of patents and other proprietary information seem to be helping China to attract more upstream R&D, as the investments mentioned suggest, but companies still have to make protecting IP a big consideration in China. Various methods are used, including stipulations in employee contracts, limiting access to sensitive technologies, and training for staff. Managing licensing rights is also important, and some companies ensure that rights are owned higher up, by the regional or home office. Particularly sensitive and innovative research is still kept in safer, more highly regulated locations by many companies. In areas where staff are in short supply, around Shanghai and Beijing, for instance, a strong staff retention programme is another way of protecting IP.

Sensitive and innovative research is still kept in safer, more highly regulated locations

We put an R&D centre here for several reasons. First of all, we wanted to have a full representation in China because China is going to be an important market, so we want to have more than just sales and marketing here. Secondly, having R&D here means we can develop Asia-specific and China-specific applications. Thirdly, in terms of basic research, if you go around the top research facilities in the world, many of the top researchers are Chinese, either overseas Chinese or people who left China after graduation to find better jobs. We wanted to create a place that would attract some of the best Chinese scholars back to China. And fourthly, R&D here can be more labour intensive, and we can leverage this to improve production costs.

Humphrey Lau, Novozymes

A wholly owned entity is the safest way to approach R&D in China. Options include expanding R&D organically within your Chinese subsidiary, or going into partnership with a university or research institute. There are government incentives ranging from zero duty on equipment to rent-free laboratories and tax relief for foreign companies setting up R&D facilities, but although running such facilities in China may look financially attractive, do not forget to take extras such as higher training and management costs into account.

China takeaways

▌ Setting up China operations is a progressive process; don't expect to do everything at once.

▌ Concentrate on quality first, which includes getting relationships with your suppliers right.

▌ Calculate unit costs carefully. Operations in China are not just about low costs and other items of production and delivery can be more expensive in terms of time and money. Instead focus on total estimated delivery costs including knowledge management.

▌ Know what knowledge you can bring to China, and what you should keep at home.

▌ Setting up in China is not just about producing, it is also about long-term thinking – how will your China operations enable you to take the next step, in China or globally?

▌ Don't underestimate the amount of senior management time that needs to be focused on these issues.

Companies setting up operations in China should have a dual strategy – to export goods or services from China and to sell within China itself. You need to be making sales where the margins are best, but you also need to be in on the fastest growing and potentially the biggest market in the world. It's time to look at the Chinese market in more detail.

References and bibliography

Kroeber, A. (2007) 'The CEQ on FT.com: Lessons for China Inc.', *Financial Times*, 20 August.

Swiss Chinese Chamber of Commerce (2005) *Behind the Kaleidoscope: A Guide to China Entry*, ch-ina.com, 448

7
Understanding and supplying the China market

The rule is, jam to-morrow and jam yesterday – but never jam to-day.

Lewis Carroll, *Alice Through the Looking Glass*

Cracking the China market is so difficult that few foreign companies, even those that have been in China for a very long time, are profitable on Chinese sales alone. China sales are seen simply as a way of covering operating costs and keeping a foot in the door. Austrian engineering firm RHI, for example, concentrates on exporting but pursues a few, high-margin sales in China, ready for when the introduction of tighter standards and stronger regulatory enforcement gives them an advantage over local competitors.

Why is the China market so difficult? Because it is not like any other market. China is certainly not the single huge market that some companies still expect to find. Scott Kronick of Ogilvy believes it takes two to three years to begin to understand the Chinese market and start selling to the Chinese, and plenty of other commentators agree.

Eventually, China should come into line with other WTO member markets, but nobody knows when that 'eventually' will arrive. If you assume that the world is converging on a standard, then do not hold your breath in China. It is more practical to operate on the assumption that China's business system, as it develops, will remain, well, Chinese and special. Yet China is potentially so important that companies are willing to play the waiting game, all the time learning more and more about operating and selling in

China. But while jam tomorrow may be a good strategy, it only works if you have the time and the budget for the long game. There are companies in China that are there primarily to supply the local market.

> Ninety-nine per cent of what we make in China, we sell in China. We didn't come here to try and access low-cost labour, we came here to pursue the Chinese market.
>
> Bill Thompson, Clyde Blowers

The success factors for selling in China look familiar — you have to know your market, know your customer, get the price right, supply your market, build a local salesforce and get paid. Let's take a look at why these are so challenging in China.

Know your market

> We see companies who bite off more than they can chew because they haven't done their homework and China is not the single, huge market they expect.
>
> Todd Rossuck, business adviser, China-Britain Business Council

There are still managers who think of China as a single market of 1.3 billion people all eagerly waiting to buy their products. They are wrong in so many ways.

> Just as there is no single cultural identity that defines a 'European', so too the Chinese cannot be lumped together as one people

In terms of area, China is almost the same size as Europe, with regions often the size of European states. And just as there is no single cultural identity that defines a 'European', so too the Chinese cannot be lumped together as one people in the sense of having the same preferences and tastes. Nobody expects the Moldovans to buy the same products in the same ways and at the same prices as the French, so why would you expect the market in Guanxi to be the same as that in Shandong? China's eastern seaboard boasts cities such as Beijing and Shanghai that are every bit as sophisticated and expensive as Paris. Head inland and Moldova's capital, Chişinău, may be a better comparison. Different cultures, dialects, even different climates mean that what works in one part of China will not work in another.

> We break it down into eight Chinas, with different influences. We see the south as being influenced by Hong Kong, the east by Japan, Korea and the US, and the west by Beijing or Guangzhou. Of course, these markets have to be researched independently, you wouldn't apply the same marketing strategy in different parts of Europe. Marketing in China has to have a geographic focus, there are different strategies for different parts of the country.
>
> Scott Kronick, Ogilvy

Differences in a glass

Scottish & Newcastle's general manager in China, Patric Dougan, described some differences between the European and Chinese markets:

- 80–85 per cent of the beer market in China is on-trade, sold in restaurants and bars rather than off-licences and supermarkets, which is very high compared with most markets.

- How products are sold can be very different. Beer in Europe is sold chilled through fonts, whereas Chinese restaurants buy beer in big bottles.

- Markets are regional rather than national because of distribution problems, and local protectionism that lingers from the past.

- Consumers are different – they like local brands and returnable bottles.

- And they're not brand-loyal. They may only drink a foreign beer when entertaining, to gain face, so getting consumer loyalty can be difficult.

- Consumer tastes also vary, and in coastal areas the beer people buy is more about status and lifestyle than further inland, where these concepts are less relevant.

- China is the biggest beer market in the world, but not the most profitable.

Critically, although marketing experts have identified sixteen product attributes, including availability, safety, brand image and composition, only two, quality and appearance, can be standardised across markets. The remaining fourteen must all be adapted to the particular market the product is aimed at, and the more market variations you have, the more possibilities there are. If we accept Ogilvy's view of eight Chinas, that's already eight markets to research. And while it may be relatively simple to get the data you need in European or US markets, it's a different story in China.

> The biggest entry barrier is to understand local sales necessities, how they behave, what they expect with the product.
>
> Gerald Kaufmann, Liaoning RHI

There are many sources of official information, which is not necessarily a good thing. The vast bureaucracy means that several departments may collect the same data, and yet they will not all give you the same results. Differences in methodology and analysis mean that data quality is sometimes suspect, and you might need to consult several sources just to form an impression about what it is you want to know. In addition, official statistics do not include any of the consumer data expected in the West – such as lifestyle, aspirational and psychographic information.

> Marketing intelligence is not that well developed. If you want very detailed, segment-by-segment and area-by-area data, it's very difficult to get. We have our own resources, and we also use the salesforce in the field. We buy a lot of studies, but the quality of those studies tends to vary a lot, and we check them against what our sales people report. We do a lot of our own research.
>
> Wangqiu Song, president, Stora Enso, China

If secondary information, that collected by other people, is unreliable and may not tell you what you need to know, then doing your own, primary, research is the key. But this can be time-consuming and expensive. Exploring fragmented and diverse markets means that research efforts have to be repeated across different areas and geographies. The speed of change means that

> The speed of change means that some types of data become obsolete very quickly

some types of data become obsolete very quickly, making the data more costly over their useful life. Then there are the Chinese themselves, whether as individuals or representatives of businesses, who tend to be wary of direct questions and may be more likely to tell you what they think you want to hear, rather than the true circumstances. As Alain Rauh, general manager of Chupa Chups in China, said, 'It is not so much the answers you get, but asking the appropriate questions that matters.' Finally, be aware that you may not actually be permitted to conduct your own research. While it could be a purely practical decision to form a partnership with a school or university, or use the contacts of your own employees, there are regulations concerning foreign invested enterprises and the use of authorised market research agencies.

However, market research is improving in China, particularly in the business-to-consumer (B2C) sector. International market research companies such as ACNielsen and TNS now operate out of Beijing, Shanghai and Guangzhou, and China-based consultancies include market research in their offerings to foreign businesses.

Using interviewers from mainland China is recommended, as they will be better placed to interpret answers, especially where cultural nuances come into play. As discussed in Chapter 5, Chinese verbal communication is high context, and a questionnaire-based interview that would be straightforward to a Western respondent may seem brusque or rude to a Chinese respondent. Obviously, this means that expats are unlikely to be directly involved in data collection, but be aware that there are circumstances where the presence of a foreigner may be helpful, such as when the status of the interviewer needs to reflect that of the interviewee. Creative use of national and local organisations, such as the All China Women's Federation, can be a good way of accessing consumers, and familiar, local organisations will be more trusted than outsiders, but remember that all associations are controlled by the party and you may have to take their results with a pinch of salt. There are now more non-govermental organisations (NGOs) operating in China, and although the CCP tries to control them, you may find they are a better source of objective information.

When developing research studies, it is advisable to incorporate internal checks into the questions, for instance by asking the same question twice in different ways so that you can compare answers, and to have supplementary, perhaps more complex, questions ready if the respondent seems willing to volunteer more information.

A nose for research

Doing your own research can mean getting down to grass roots. Todd Rossuck, a business adviser with the China-Britain Business Council, spent fourteen years in China working as sales director and general manager of International Flavours and Fragrances.

'We carried out a research project on fragrances in the mid-1980s. At the time, most rural Chinese used soap bars made from animal fats which had no added fragrance and, to us at least, smelled horrible. There was a tremendous opportunity to bring fragranced synthetic soaps and detergents to consumers, but we didn't know how they would react to these new products.

'Much of our research relied on finding a way to go directly to the consumer, whether through organised groups or simply by contacting housewives known to our salespeople. For this project, our office manager in Guangzhou used her contacts in the Sichuan government, and through them we made arrangements to visit a number of villages in Sichuan province. A small team of us would literally arrive at someone's house, set up buckets of warm water, demonstrate the soap or detergent powder, and introduce the fragrance. We would soon have a crowd of children watching, and labourers would come in from the fields to see what was going on.

'Unexpectedly, it was sometimes hard for the villagers to even recognise that there was a fragrance at all, especially if it was a fine, floral fragrance – perhaps because the food in Sichuan is so hot and spicy. So our questions to the villagers started with, "Can you smell the fragrance?" before we went on to ask if they liked it.'

Business-to-business data is more difficult to obtain. Access to many factories is challenging and answers tend to reflect the official line, rather than what is actually happening.

Foreign companies with big budgets have sometimes been able to solve this problem by buying market knowledge, hiring people who have the specific knowledge they need or even taking over companies in the right sector or location.

As with everything else in China, you must do due diligence on all the secondary and primary research that you carry out. Anecdotal evidence must be cross-checked, as must statistics from official sources, and ensure that any experts you consult are up to date. Writing in the *China Business Review* in 2004, Charles Oliver and John E. Coulter came up with Table 7.1 to show how the uses and values of information vary depending on what is being researched.

Table 7.1 Value of information source by type of information in China (1 = not useful; 5 = very useful)

Type of information	Anecdotal	Experts	Inside guanxi	Secondary sources	Systematic primary
General market trends	4	3	3	2	5
Demographics	1	1	1	5	1
Market opportunities	2	2	3	1	5
Partner search	2	1	3	1	5
Market size, share	2	1	1	2	5
Regulations	2	3	1	4	2
Project information	1	3	3	2	4
Competitive analysis	2	2	2	1	5
Detailed price information	2	2	1	2	5

Source: 'China Market Research Strategies', Charles Oliver and John E. Coulter, *China Business Review*, May–June 2004 chapter 4 doc 13042916

Clearly, systematic, primary research is the answer for most types of investigation. If you're serious about tackling China properly, you will have to include this in your budgetary considerations.

Researching the China market

▌ Conduct primary research.

▌ Use the right interviewers for the target group.

▌ Do due diligence on all data, primary and especially secondary.

▌ Accept 'defeat' when your research shows that the Chinese will not buy your products.

▌ Don't leave your brain on the plane! The same rigour – sample size, amount of data needed to support a decision, etc – should be applied to research in China as anywhere else, it may just take longer and be more expensive to get the information you need.

Once the research is done, the data analysis and conclusions must keep the Chinese context in mind. Apparently familiar types of data should perhaps not be viewed in the same way as in Europe or the US. Disposable income must be balanced against the Chinese propensity to save as much money as possible, so what seems like increased spending power may actually translate into greater savings.

You must also be aware of the big picture of what is happening in China. Recent scares over contaminated and sub-standard foods

> Recent scares have made Chinese consumers wary about what they buy

and medicines, which in some cases have led to deaths, have made Chinese consumers wary about what they buy. According to Scottish and Newcastle's Patric Dougan, 'The average Chinese shopper in a supermarket spends four times as long reading labels as they do in the West.'

Know your customer

We have a narrow customer portfolio of five segments of the population, but we don't apply the same profile everywhere we go. We know that the perceptions of customers regarding value, brand, service and quality differ from city to city – we need to show different faces in some cities to others. I'd say there's probably a 70:30 split between the national brand and local adaptations, which takes account of the fact that customers in a particular location have different requirements.

Mark Ladham, retail managing director, B&Q, China

Knowing your customer is critical, otherwise you won't be able to interpret research data correctly. As China changes, so too do your customers, so understanding them is not just about how they are now, but also how their tastes and needs might change in the future, and this applies equally whether your business is B2B or B2C.

Our customers are constantly changing. They're asking things now they would never have thought of asking ten years ago. Their businesses are getting bigger and their knowledge and competency are improving all the time.

LiLi, Novozymes

The research does not stop once you've identified your customer base. Especially for products that are new to China, there is tremendous scope to expand your company by developing your customers.

Understanding and developing your customers – B2B

Enzymes and micro-organisms are used in more than forty industries, including the production of textiles, food and detergents, but when Danish enzyme company Novozymes went to China, it had to overcome a lack of knowledge and outdated, chemicals-based production processes. Novozymes used several tactics to persuade customers that enzymes could replace chemicals, increase equipment lifetime through requiring less extreme temperature and pressure conditions, and be better for the environment.

We had to create our markets, because nobody was using enzymes in their processes, they were all using chemicals. It took us several years. We had to demonstrate the products, which we did through risk-sharing deals with selected customers. We gave them free samples, sometimes we even had to buy the raw materials for them as well. They did the trials and then we told other companies about the results through industry associations. We targeted the textile, detergent and starch catalysation industries. It was a big investment, but within three years, one hundred and thirty factories had switched from chemical processes to enzyme processes, that's a lot of business for us.

LiLi, sales director, Novozymes

The challenge is to find and understand your customer in the first place, and then grow with them as their appetite for products and services develops. Once you have identified a starting point in China, remember that relationships must be established with potential customers before business can begin. Local government and local and national industry associations are valuable sources of information and contacts, and foreign trade organisations hold meetings and events where businesses can meet each other. Don't underestimate the importance of 'meeting and greeting' potential customers and helping them to gain face. Overseas trips to visit your headquarters or manufacturing plants and meetings with the MD and other senior managers when they are in China are two important ways in which you can publicly demonstrate the importance of your customer.

It's very hard to build customer loyalty. You have to make them feel like they are your most important customer, that you give them the best service and the best price. But they communicate with each other, they find out how often your technical people visit and they compare prices. When the boss comes from Denmark, we take him to visit customers to make them feel important, sometimes we invite our customers to visit the US or Denmark. But even then, if they find a price just a few per cent lower than yours, they'll switch. I've just had to fly to visit a customer and try to persuade them not to switch to one of our competitors. The customer says he's getting a big discount, but I had to find out what else he was being offered. And then I have to realise that he might not be telling me the truth – 80 per cent I trust, 20 per cent I check.

LiLi, sales director, Novozymes

Companies in the B2B sector find that bigger customers tend to have greater experience of dealing with foreign companies and act more 'professionally' from a Western perspective, but also have greater bargaining power because of their size and position in the market. Smaller companies may be harder to develop a relationship with initially, but working with them could be a good way to get started.

Understanding and developing your customers: B2C

Ikea has learnt not only about what its Chinese customers like to buy, but also about how culture and attitudes affect purchases. Some lessons were very basic – the company originally attempted to sell 'Hong Kong-size' beds, but soon realised that these were too short for mainland Chinese. Ikea also found that DIY, including the type of self-assembly for which the company is noted, was not popular. Ikea solved this by offering a fee-based assembly service. Other lessons have had more complex messages. Research into which areas of their homes the Chinese liked to spend money on found that the living room came first. This is logical in a country where face is important – the living room is for entertaining guests, and much entertainment in China is about giving and receiving face. Ikea also found that the Chinese had an all-or-nothing attitude towards decorating, which turned home improvement into a major and expensive project. The company began educating customers in the notion of step changes, adding to the home a little at a time.

Source: Paula M. Miller, 'Ikea with Chinese characteristics', *China Business Review*, July–August 2004

If you intend to sell to consumers via third-party distributors, do not assume that the same type of distributor will work as well in China as elsewhere. Providers of healthcare and personal care products might normally expect to sell via supermarkets, but supermarket shopping is still relatively new and the Chinese are more accustomed to buying such products in a chemist's shop.

We'll have another look at customers as consumers in the next chapter, when we discuss brands and how you market products to consumers who have little or no brand loyalty.

Get the price right

A high-status brand can price things more aggressively, but then the products have to live up to the expectations that go with the stronger brand. It is all about knowing your market, the local dynamics and the competition.

Scott Kronick, President China Ogilvy PR

Getting away from competing on price is one of the biggest problems for foreign companies in China. You cannot match prices with local competitors and hope to survive – they can always go a bit lower than you, and they can always cut a few more corners to eke out their margins.

In the mainstream beer business in China, profits come from having very high market share in one region, that's where you can get economies of scale and some pricing power.

Dougan, GM and China Business Development Director, Scottish & Newcastle Asia (S&N)

Savings achieved through producing goods more cheaply may disappear once you start to consider increased transportation costs

Savings achieved through producing goods more cheaply may disappear once you start to consider increased transportation costs (see below), relocation expenses for expatriates, training for local staff (including overseas trips to see how things are done elsewhere in the company) and the time that must be devoted to building relationships. Worse still, as has been discussed, copies of your products could be available at much lower prices a very short time after launch, courtesy of the local competition. While you have to factor in many additional costs in your pricing strategy, Chinese firms will be able to undercut you with impunity.

This is why companies are advised to adopt a dual strategy towards China – sell locally and export, which adds to your pricing headache. Production quality will be crucial for your exports, but can you afford to sell the same quality of product in China? If not, does that mean you will have to run two production lines, one for local sales and one for exports? What message will that send to your Chinese staff, and via them to their family, friends and the wider community?

Getting the price right is a critical part of your China strategy, but one that will require a great deal of thought. If you're selling to consumers, what you might consider a 'normal' price will almost certainly be too high for the mid- to low-end, volume markets. If you're selling to other businesses, their quality requirements will play a large role in how you price your products.

> As our customers get bigger, their bargaining power gets greater. They can put a downward pressure on prices and we have to adjust elsewhere, for instance improving productivity and supply processes.
>
> LiLi, Novozymes

Some companies work on the strategy that using aggressive pricing will help them gain market share in China, assuming that if they can keep prices low enough, the competition will have less room to manoeuvre. To do this, the foreign company almost certainly has to sell its older products rather than the latest technology, and this is becoming less acceptable to purchasers in a rapidly developing China where consumer awareness of quality is rising. This strategy clearly has budgetary implications – again, it's a case of jam tomorrow – and not all firms will be able to price in this way. Businesses with smaller subsidiaries in China will not be able to achieve the economies of scale necessary to keep prices down and will have to find other ways of attracting buyers.

Supply your market

> With pricing being relatively low, and distribution costs and infrastructure in China being high relative to value, the rate for economically rational distribution of a mainstream beer in China is a maximum 400km, probably more like 300km.
>
> Patric Dougan, Scottish & Newcastle

Many companies are advised to start small in China, choose one or two cities and get established before venturing further afield. One of the reasons behind this is the problem of distribution. We've talked about China being several markets depending on geography and local culture, but distribution costs and challenges also contribute to the regional variations in selling your products in China. Although companies such as FedEx and DHL have made great progress in China in recent years, getting goods from A to B still depends on where B is. The regional and provincial autonomy that affects so much else in business also gives rise to local protectionism, typically seen in non-tariff barriers related to factors that local governments control, which means that distributing and selling goods from one factory across provinces is expensive and unpredictable.

The Maoist doctrine of encouraging self-reliance among cities and provinces means that transporting goods from, say, Beijing to Shanghai could involve going through several provincial and municipal borders, with their accompanying mountains of paperwork and multifarious fees. As one commentator wrote (Powers, 2001), in the past 'firms [were] forced ... to use highly creative methods to bypass anachronistic and restrictive regulations in order to distribute their products'. Things are changing now, although as with so much in China, the nearer you are to the eastern seaboard, the more these changes will be apparent.

VERMONT CAREER GATEWAY

To cope with the rising demand for products to be distributed around China, the government is rapidly expanding the road and railway networks. The National Bureau of Statistics of China reported 46,000km of new roads in 2004, 129,748km in 2005, and 93,720km in 2006. Railway construction amounted to some 2,000km in 2004, 2,552km in 2005 and more than 6,000km in 2006. Over the same period, waterways have continued to play an important role, accounting for 11–12 per cent of all freight carried, with railways responsible for about 14 per cent and roads responsible for approximately 72 per cent (the remainder being divided between air freight and pipelines). In 2006, over 20 billion tons of freight were shipped within China.

But despite the massive transport infrastructure programme, much of the investment is going into primary networks, and getting goods to their final destination, usually involving secondary and perhaps tertiary routes, is not straightforward. Reaching customers even in

> Reaching customers even in some of the bigger cities often means that products end up on the back of a motorised tricycle

some of the bigger cities often means that products end up on the back of a motorised tricycle for the final phase of their journey, so goods that leave the factory in a container will have to be packaged to withstand at least one and probably several transfers, from one size of container to another and from one form of transport to another. For products such as beer, this can result in high breakage rates.

Because of the contrast between primary and secondary transportation routes in China, you cannot simply copy Western distribution methods. Transport and logistics will have to be adapted to the local situation, and this may include new packaging and loading methods. In particular, additional quality checks may be needed when goods have to be switched from one mode of transport to another, as the more the goods are handled, the greater the risk of damage.

Not surprisingly, therefore, transportation in China can be inefficient, slow and expensive. Writing in the *China Business Review* in 2004, Alberto Nogales and Graham Smith, transport specialists with the World Bank, estimated that transportation in China accounted for about half of total logistics costs, roughly double that in developed countries.

For B2C companies, another aspect of supplying the market is identifying where a consumer is going to buy your product. As mentioned earlier, retail pharmacies may be a better outlet for personal and healthcare products than supermarkets. But because they may not have sophisticated inventory systems, you may have to provide or develop such a system with retail pharmacy partners to manage inventory more efficiently. Other distribution methods can involve more direct charges:

> To have a significant presence in the beer market, you have to pay listing fees in bars. If you've got a full portfolio of drinks, then maybe it starts to make sense to do that. But everyone is chasing the same outlets and everyone is paying a lot of money to the outlets. In some cases it's for guaranteed volume, in others, simply for the right to sell your products.
>
> Patric Dougan, Scottish & Newcastle

Build a local salesforce

> Selling as a local company is very different from selling as an importer, sales channels are very different, you need to build a local salesforce.
>
> Gerald Kaufmann, Liaoning RHI

Your local salesforce will be critical in learning about and developing your customers. Selling in China is less difficult if your product is different from local products, but it is much harder if similar Chinese products are available, not least because price competition will be stiff. For this reason, you need to develop products for the local market, and to do this you will need close, frequent contacts with customers. A local salesforce will be able to build the kind of personal relationship with potential customers that will help you to understand what level of products your customers will buy.

> ## Understanding Chinese culture is very much implied in the selling process

On another level, understanding Chinese culture is very much implied in the selling process. It would be foolish to expect that you could bring in a group of expatriate salesmen and watch them make sales, however good they are in their home country, because none of the home rules apply and they will make mistakes from day one. As Patric Dougan of Scottish & Newcastle said, 'You can fly in technical experts, that's fine, but the closer you get to the consumer, the more you need to know about the region and the market.'

Your salespeople will have to develop in two directions – they will need to learn more about your customers, and also more about what is going on in your industry. Increasing awareness among both business customers and consumers, along with greater availability of information on the World Wide Web, makes it more of a challenge to be one step ahead of your customers' needs.

> One of the big challenges is to grow with your customers and our salespeople are an important part of that. Nowadays, they don't only have to know about the products, but also about what is happening elsewhere. Customers in China want to know what our European customers are doing, what our competition is doing, and the salespeople have to know the big picture.
>
> LiLi, Novozymes

Everything that you learnt about people in Chapter 5 will be doubly important for your salesforce. They will possess commercially valuable knowledge not only about your products but also about your customers, and robust retention strategies for your salesforce will be vital.

Direct selling – a different approach

Shaklee is a 52-year-old direct-selling company that sells nutritional products, environmentally friendly home-cleaning products and cosmetics and personal care items through a network of individual distributors. John Holden, former chairman of Shaklee China, believes that the direct-selling model works well for China, where an extra income, especially for older people laid off from state enterprises who have little education or capital, is welcome. But direct selling in China has a chequered history – early entrants Avon and Amway faced few regulations because direct selling was new to China, but by 1998, the government feared home-grown pyramid schemes had come to see such operations as fronts for organised religion and other subversive groups and banned direct selling (see Chapter 3 for the Amway story). Shaklee started negotiations with the Ministry of Commerce in 2005 and finally received a licence in March 2007. It is the only company that has been licensed for direct selling that was not operating in China before the 1998 clampdown and the authorities have not granted any new licences since May 2007. Salespeople are not directly employed, but Shaklee provides them with the opportunity to work part-time or full-time, and salespeople range from those doing it for pin money to those who see selling as a route to a good income.

Get paid

The Chinese are very good at getting money into China, but they think that money should not leave China, once it is here.

Keith Linch, Robinson JZFZ

'Collection is more important than sales,' I was told when researching this book. The UK Trade & Investment (UKTI) factsheet 'Getting Paid' starts with the discouraging words, 'The least risky option for selling to China (or indeed to anyone) is to seek advanced payment in full.' As far as I am aware, it is only the consumer who pays in advance in full, just before they pick up their carrier bags of shopping and head to their car. Selling B2B, or to consumers via distributors, is not so simple.

There is definitely an attitude that Chinese business customers don't pay, which some put down to underhandedness but others, more correctly, attribute to the fact that doing business in China is different. We described the Confucian system of relationships that underlies Chinese culture in Chapter 5, and a foreign company, especially one that hasn't been in China very long, is part of the out-group and so essentially 'fair game'. Family comes first, and it is only the exceptional foreigner – Henry Kissinger, for example – who can ever hope to be treated as something more than an outsider.

Given that you will be low in the pecking order of who will be looked after first, it is crucial to establish strategies to survive what could be very long payment schedules, if indeed a 'schedule' exists at all. The first step is to do due diligence on customers. Among other things, you need to check their reputation, trading record and ability to pay. Payment terms should be included in any signed agreements. The UKTI recommends the documentary letter of credit as 'the tried, tested, preferred and least risky way of securing payment from new customers'.

Other recommendations include not supplying goods until they are paid for, holding a second shipment until payment is received for the previous one, offering large discounts for early payment and, inevitably, using *guanxi* relationships to put pressure on late payers. More creative solutions may also be necessary, such as finding an alternative payer, which may be a subsidiary or associate of the company you are dealing with. Things can get even more complicated as foreign companies adopt 'Chinese-style' strategies towards their own creditors. A powdered milk company was presented with a large tax bill, but since it was owed money by several customers, the milk company said it could not afford the tax. A compromise was reached whereby the milk company paid

> A compromise was reached whereby the milk company paid the salaries of local teachers

the salaries of local teachers, which was equivalent to half the tax bill, and the local authorities cancelled the rest of the tax.

> We use people from the UK to do design work for our China projects, so it is similar to consultancy. We set up the contracts with our parent company back in the UK to provide consultancy services in China, and they invoice us monthly. We have to apply for a foreign exchange licence to convert our RMB into sterling and then we pay the invoices.
>
> Keith Linch, Robinson JZFZ

Export

Whatever your sales strategy within China, you may have to export, and this will have a bearing on all aspects of your China operations. Take Danfoss, the Danish group. When it entered China, it supplied three types of customers: global clients abroad (through Wuqing exports), global OEMs (original equipment manufacturers) in China and domestic Chinese producers (through a combination of imports and local output). The majority of Danfoss goods sold on the domestic market were still imported from other plants abroad. Initially, the Wuqing plant sold nearly all its output abroad, which helped to buy time to build up relationships with international customers producing in China, and to start to build up the domestic market.

The targeting of both the domestic and export markets was key to Wuqing's success, ensuring, early on, the volumes necessary to get costs down and quality up. 'Exporting, from the outset, meant we could start, with a relatively high scale, serving customers outside China,' explained Helberg, then global head of the refrigeration and air-conditioning segment. 'We weren't dependent on a market that wasn't yet there. The dual strategy also boosted Danfoss marketing worldwide.' As Daisy Xu, supply chain manager noted, Danfoss penetration of large, globalising Chinese manufacturers might, in the longer run, help it expand in the US market, by 'coming with them to the US'. And success in China benefited sales in the rest of the world. 'Increasingly, as a global company, we are being asked by our customers to fulfil their needs, whether they are in Asia-Pacific or in other parts of the world,' said Carsten Sørensen, president of Danfoss China. 'Our factory in Tianjin is a huge asset for our business…across the globe.'

Nonetheless, in the context of this chapter, even though you probably know your home markets intimately, the fact that you are sourcing goods from China will have an effect. Given the product recalls and scandals that seem to come to light every year, you may find that customers are wary about buying goods labelled 'made in China'. You may need to bring B2B customers to your factories to see how you ensure that quality standards and regulations are met, and perhaps offer a trial with your products.

Similarly, the news about port development in China is impressive, but there are hitches too, which you'll have to account for. Prodigious growth in port facilities illustrates the maritime and trading thrust of Chinese policy. China's ports are concentrated in three regions: the Pearl river delta (Shenzen, Guangzhou), the Yangtze river delta (Shanghai, Ningbo), Bohai (Qingdao, Tianjin, Dalian). These seven ports account for 70 per cent of China's national throughput, the regions themselves contributing to 60 per cent of China's GDP. Over five years, bulk volume traffic through Chinese ports (excluding Hong Kong) rose from 1.4 billion tons in 2001 to 3.1 billion tons in 2005, an average 20 per cent year-on-year increase over five years. The growth in containerised activity is even more spectacular, with volumes tripling from 27 million TEU (20-foot equivalent units) in 2001 to 75 million TEU in 2005. The goals for port development under the eleventh five-year plan are to attain a port traffic volume of 7.5 billion tons of bulk cargo by 2010 (more than double current volumes), and a container traffic volume of 130–150 billion TEU. Cargo turnover at the Shanghai port exceeded 500 million tons in 2006, making it the world's busiest port for the second consecutive year. The seven greatest Chinese ports mentioned above rank within the top thirty container harbours in the world. China is rising rapidly with the efficiency which its ports are used, raising its attraction as an investment location.

These statistics are impressive, and a long-term intention of the Chinese leadership is to develop China as maritime power. But for the moment, and your viewpoint, it is as well to remember that shipping has quality and logistics implications. As described above, lack of integration between transport systems in China means that goods often have to be unloaded and reloaded to transfer them from one mode to another, which presents the possibility of damage. Ikea takes steps to avoid risking transporting damaged goods, sometimes holding inspections at consolidation points where goods are loaded into containers for shipment overseas. Another cause of shipping bottlenecks was a change in VAT rules, when companies suddenly needed to ship goods out quickly to meet a deadline for VAT rebates, so there are bigger picture, contextual issues to watch as well as what is happening within your own company and with your suppliers.

A challenge for exporters from China is capacity at the ports, particularly at busy periods when many companies are competing for space on ships. Shipping managers have to try and guess when other companies will ship their products and plan accordingly, but as Ikea's Michael Sagan says, 'If you guess the same way as, say, Wal-Mart, then you're really creating a big bottleneck.' And don't forget the other end – some US ports, for example, are not capable of handling large quantities of imports in a timely and efficient manner.

Coupled with the physical challenge of shipping at the right time is that of pricing. While the price with your supplier may be agreed, shipping prices can fluctuate according to time and demand, so co-ordinating timing, delivery and costs is complex.

China takeaways

▌ Familiar success factors apply when understanding and supplying Chinese customers – know your market, know your customer, get the price right, supply your market, get paid and build a local salesforce – but the reality of doing business in China makes them far more challenging to get right than in your home market.

▌ Research, research, research if you want to learn how to supply Chinese customers.

▌ Remember that sales aren't sales until the money is safely in your account.

▌ Go into China with a dual sales strategy – domestic and export – so your operation is not reliant on a new and unpredictable market.

▌ Don't forget to key a sharp eye on the development of China's infrastructure, and particularly its transport system. It's impressive, but so is China's growth.

▌ Remember, Chinese customers are very demanding and seek quality for a good price.

> The Chinese beer market landscape is littered with corpses of brands that launched and spent a lot of money and disappeared.
>
> Patric Dougan, Scottish & Newcastle

If you can't compete on price in China, then you have to look to your brand for a competitive advantage. It's now time to see how companies tackle branding in a country where consumers are fickle and brand loyalty is a relatively new concept.

References and bibliography

Nogales, A., and Smith, G. (2004) 'China's evolving transportation sector', *China Business Review*, Mar/Apr, pp.24–9.

Powers, P. (2001) 'Distribution in China: The end of the beginning,' *China Business Review*, July–August 2001.

Promoting the brand

Wisdom is sold in the desolate market where none come to buy.

William Blake

Chinese consumers are fiercely loyal to their favourite brands. Chinese consumers never buy the same brand twice. Both these statements are true, which is why you have to work extremely hard in China to understand your market and your customers if you are going to build a brand in China. Companies that attempt to transport their foreign brand model lock, stock and barrel into China are asking for trouble. Recent business history in China is littered with disasters, from brand names translated as 'shit' (or worse) to Peugeot insulting the Chinese by attempting to sell them old models. Just as property buyers are urged to focus on three things – location, location, location – companies wishing to establish their brands should also focus on three things – research, research, research – if they are going to gain the kind of wisdom that will keep them out of Blake's 'desolate market'.

While there's nothing certain in life apart from death and taxes, in China there's nothing certain in business apart from change, so the research you do to determine how to establish your brand will merely be the start of a process. Not only do you have to keep abreast of rapidly changing customer preferences as the Chinese are exposed to more products, but you must also watch an evolving media, burgeoning sales channels, regulatory frameworks, growing customer income and spending power, and a fast and furious competitive landscape. This chapter aims to give a glimpse of the thinking that must underpin your brand strategy decisions in

China. It will look at that loyal-disloyal creature, the Chinese consumer, and discuss the importance of localising and extending brands and what you need to know before allocating your brand-building budget. But first, let's take a look at the party-state's own information policy, and the transformation of China's media scene.

China in the global knowledge structure

The information technology revolution lies at the heart of the party-state's ambition to turn China into a technological powerhouse. The statistics show that the party-state has been extremely successful. The result is a population that is better informed than ever before. Take the print industry first. Official statistics show Chinese readers in 1978 had 930 magazines, 186 newspapers, and 14,987 book titles to choose from; by 2006, official statistics recorded 9,468 magazines and trade publications; 1,938 newspapers, and 233,971 book titles selling 64 billion copies. Similarly, in 1978, every 100 urban families had only 0.59 colour TV sets; by 2006, with over 59 million urban households surveyed in the urban areas of China, that figure had risen to 137 colour TV sets. By then, 100 urban households owned an average of 47 computers, and 153 mobile phones. By 2007, mobile phone users numbered 547 million. In terms of internet users, the total number at the end of 2008 was about 253 million and growing at 53 per cent a year. The government intent is to bring broadband and multimedia access to all urban homes by 2010. The rural world is also being networked into the information society. Rapid growth is recorded of internet use in rural areas, spurred on by government policies such as 'every village has access to internet' and 'every village has a website'.

This networking of China challenges the party to adapt its policies of control over the media to the fast-changing technologies its policies have unleashed. Until the late 1990s, the regime's information policy followed Mao's precept whereby the media were to function as the party's 'loyal eyes, ears and tongue'. They were tools for the party-state to impose ideological hegemony on society, and to popularise government policies. Control over the system was tight, and under the direct leadership of the party-state in Beijing. Local supervision came from provincial, municipal and local party propaganda departments, and the provincial or municipal broadcasting administrative bureau. Technological, regulatory and administrative affairs were under government tutelage. Open debate on ideology was not allowed, and media criticism of the party-state and its high-ranking officials, policies and affairs were punished. Self-imposed censorship was widespread, and every individual in the media knew what and what not to do. Important editorials, news stories and sensitive programmes all required advance endorsement by the party authorities.

This legacy has not been discarded. What has changed are the policies, which are designed to strengthen government controls. The military, the police, the party and the Ministry of Information Industry (MII) – a giant composite ministry, with its own operating companies brought together in 1998 – invest massively in telecommunications and data-processing to centralise control and monitor the population. Web use is encouraged for business and educational purposes, but the government tries to block access to pornographic sites or to what it considers as subversive material. An ever-expanding army of online censors, numbering 50,000 and based in Beijing, run an internet filtering system, oversee web browsing through broadband access points, and police emails, chat rooms, blogs and internet cafés. Internet users have to sign on to an official register. In 2002, some three hundred members of the internet industry – Sina, Sohu, NetEase, Renmin and Xinhau among others – signed a public pledge on self-discipline. Foreign media remain under central surveillance, while local journalists face restrictions on their work. In the 2008 'press freedom index' – assembled by Reporters Without Frontiers, an international NGO campaigning for press freedom – China ranked 163 out of the 169 countries on its list, in the company of such countries as Vietnam, Burma and Iran.

You may conclude that it's best to steer clear of 'politics'. You'd be wrong. For starters, the party-state is omnipresent; you cannot stay clear of it. What is more, party-state officials decide what is or is not 'politics', not you. Consider the case of Avon, the direct sales cosmetics group. Avon had lobbied Beijing for permission to develop its business, but found the process unrewarding, and headed for the provinces. Guangdong authorities were receptive, and the company began to roll out its plans for door-to-door sales. Others soon followed Avon's example, so that by 1997 there were about 2,300 direct-selling firms in China, employing up to twenty million people and generating a sales volume of $2 billion (Chan, 1999). But the State Council in April 1998 issued a blanket ban. All door-to-door sales operations were ordered to convert to standard retail distribution or go out of business. The official reason for the clampdown was that hundreds of thousands of consumers had been ripped off in scams that had swept the country. The unofficial reason was that party bureaucrats thought the rituals used to arouse the enthusiasm of the sales teams at marketing meetings were too much like religious revivalist movements. Avon had to concede, and swiftly altered its business model to open shops. The decision was reversed by the Commerce Ministry in early 2006, after the government decided to reintroduce direct sales, with a law undertaking a stricter regulation of the sector. Avon China chief executive Andrea Jung evaluated the measure's potential contribution to the company's bottom line at $1 billion.

The lesson from Avon's story is that it pays to divine what China's collective emperor is thinking, especially when it comes to the information industry.

> As we have no immediate experience of what other men feel, we can form no idea of the manner in which they are affected, but by conceiving what we ourselves should feel in the like situation.

> Adam Smith, *The Theory of Moral Sentiments* (1759)

As Adam Smith advised, it's wise to make a leap of imagination, with the help of some information. The information is that the party-state has shifted its media policy from one of propaganda to redefining the role of the media as one of agenda-setting. This is because a growing diversity of information sources obliges the party-state to provide credible information in an ever more open society. It can no longer control public opinion and rule the media, but has to settle for guidance and supervision.

The web in particular has become a prominent forum where the public can, and does, make known its opinions to the government.

This enables the party leadership to build a more direct bridge to public opinion, over the heads of tiers of government officials. Under the new dispensation, the people's voice is given expression, especially when local government officials are being criticised, or when central government directives have not been adequately implemented. One out of countless examples of how Beijing uses the media for its own purposes is the explosion that occurred in November 2005 at a petrochemical plant in Jilin City. The blast produced a spill, estimated at 100 tons of toxic substances, into the Songhua river. In the weeks that followed, contamination of water supplies affected residents from rural north-eastern China, including the provincial capital of Harbin and all the way to the Russian frontier. Beijing indulged in its secrecy habit, and allowed ten days to pass before notifying Harbin residents of the situation. The excuse for the delay was to avoid panic, but the media attacked local government officials for the cover-up. Beijing's official position was expressed in a report on the spill by a United Nations Environment Programme team, whereby central government instructions were not adequately communicated to the public. 'Had this communication been adequately provided, the level of uncertainty and fear by the public would have been lower,' said the Environmental News Service.

Why, you may well ask, is the party-state encouraging the development of an information society that challenges its powers to control opinion? The answer is simple enough: it wants to build a huge internal market, and make China a leading centre of innovation. Keeping track of public opinion is important, but no less important is the party-state's determination to ensure a stream of revenues from its lucrative businesses. There are fewer more remunerative than the media industry. In the early 1990s, Beijing launched three 'golden projects': an electronic infrastructure for the conveyance of economic information; a 'golden card' system to create a payment clearance system for banks; and a 'golden customs' project to speed up customs clearance. A matrix was constructed of eight cables running east-west and eight running north-south. From 2000, the party-state backed media enterprises trying to raise capital from domestic or foreign sources. A 'government-online' policy was also launched. The result has been an expanding communications infrastructure, party-state promotion of concentration in the media industry, and the emergence of media groups that fall under the tutelage, direct or indirect, of the *very* powerful MII.

Just how lucrative China's media market is can be seen in the statistics: the state-run seven o'clock news has 500 million viewers – the most watched programme in the world. Broadcast TV, which accounts for 60 per cent of all media revenues, is reckoned in 2006 as having 1.2 billion viewers above the age of four. In that year, the top ten provincial media markets, including the big three of Beijing, Shanghai and Guandong, accounted for 90 per cent of all media revenue – indicating the highly uneven development of the media across the country, but also the potential. Sichuan, for instance, is the largest TV market in western China, and growing fast, while Hunan satellite TV is now a market leader nationwide, with advertising revenues of over RMB1.2 billion in 2007. But the fastest-growing segments of China's media markets are the internet and digital media. As Peter Lovelock, director of the Telecoms Research Project, points out, digital technology is changing the media landscape, led by Chinese and foreign media companies (KPMG, 2008). 'Across an ever increasing array of devices and formats, advertisers and marketers are increasingly able to target and engage consumers.' It's time to look more closely at Chinese consumers.

The Chinese consumer

The key challenge for foreign brands in China…is somehow achieving a balance between broad accessibility and premium image.

Tom Doctoroff, J. Walter Thomson

Your understanding of the apparently schizophrenic nature of Chinese consumers when it comes to brands lies in understanding their culture. Brands that are seen, that demonstrate status, are the

Brands that demonstrate status are the ones that evoke fierce loyalty

ones that evoke fierce loyalty, and these include luxury products and high-end home furnishings and appliances. The watch brand Omega is immensely successful in China, having captured 70 per cent of the men's luxury watch market. The booming market in counterfeits of prestige brands also points to how keen the Chinese are to have such items on display.

Brands that don't matter because they aren't used to mark status, for example food and other commodities, have a much harder time developing loyalty because, when everything else is the same, the consumer will buy based on price. This problem is compounded by the level of choice available – it is much more difficult to differentiate a product when it is lined up in the supermarket with thiry or forty equivalent products.

Yet both luxury and commodity brands can be successful in China, it's simply a question of understanding the market, understanding your customer, getting the positioning just right, distributing your products in a way that is consistent with their brand image, and making sure your marketing activities tie in and support everything else. Easy.

> Our brand is consistent. We are an international brand, our strength is to differentiate in terms of service, quality, transparency of price. All those things should and do differentiate us from the local competition.
>
> Mark Ladham, B&Q

Let's start with shopping behaviour in China. You won't be surprised to hear that it is different from that of typical Western consumers. A 2003 report pointed out that one-third of visitors to a Chinese shopping centre did not buy anything (Li *et al.*). Cultural values of frugality and diligence mean that, when planning to make a big purchase, the Chinese gather as much information about the product as possible before they buy, so shopping is as much about gathering information as it is about buying.

Paradoxically, this meticulous approach makes the Chinese open to point-of-purchase marketing. Once they have done all the background research on, say, television sets, the Chinese consumer will have an overall view of the type of TV they are interested in. But since the majority of Chinese consumers are not yet loyal to any brand, when they are ready to make the purchase, it is unlikely that they will go to the store to buy a specific TV. Instead, the best deal on the day will probably win. From a cultural point of view, this shows the importance of relationships in Chinese society extends to buying, because a well-trained shop assistant who can quickly develop a relationship with potential customers will have the edge. So you would be wise to look on branding in terms of how you build a relationship between your products, your customers and your company.

> The Chinese beer market is 'push' based – consumers tend to buy the beer that is pushed by the retailers and wholesalers. We want to move it towards a 'pull' based model, a more branded market where consumers pick the beer they like.
>
> Eric Melloul, China director of marketing, InBev

The idea of relationships is also seen in research that suggests it is intangibles that attract the Chinese consumer. China is a high context society, as mentioned before, and relationships help build the context, in this case the links between your customer and your product. A 2003 McKinsey survey into how people bought cars noted that only two of the top ten attributes cited by purchasers were about the vehicle itself, the other eight all reflected how the car would make the owner feel or how it would position the owner in his or her circle of family and friends (Hoffe *et al.*).

Intangibles drive purchasing behaviour

Top ten attributes that lead car buyers in China to make their purchase:

1	For people like me.
2	Attractive styling.
3	Friends say it's a good car.
4	A pleasure to drive.
5	Good maintenance record/rarely breaks down.
6	A good family car.
7	Reliable.
8	Makes me feel safe.
9	Makes me feel attractive/successful.
10	Manufacturer is industry leader.*

*Although industry leadership was most important to 61 per cent of buyers, it was so unimportant to the other 39 per cent that it dropped to tenth of seventy-eight attributes.

Source: Hoffe *et al.* (2003)

However, there are conflicting views on this, with others pointing out that complexity can be a good selling point for items such as cameras, which may be proudly put on display on a coffee table and the technical bells and whistles carefully pointed out to those the owner wishes to impress. Ultimately, this is about doing your own research – customers in Shanghai will have different attitudes towards brands than those in cities inland, and you will have to focus on your value propositions accordingly, an emotional appeal may work in Shanghai, but a functional appeal may work better in Xi'an. If, however, you are aiming at the teenage market, you may find greater similarities across geographies than among the generations.

Incomes are rising and so is spending. Deloitte reported that consumer spending in 2003 amounted to some $1.1 trillion, with 41 per cent of that spent on food, and $56 billion on clothing. While incomes and spending continue to grow, so do savings. The Chinese save because they cannot trust the government to provide the medical care that they may need, or look after them in their old age – history has shown them that safety nets, like the iron rice bowl, can be removed without notice. The Chinese are, therefore,

The Chinese are still very conscious of price

still very conscious of price, hence their tendency to do research on big purchases and a willingness to take a good deal rather than a preferred brand. So beware the thinking that building a brand will enable you to charge a premium. Sony is able to charge a 40 per cent premium in some markets, but in China, even a 10 per cent premium over a local brand loses them market share. McKinsey research (Hoffe *et al.*) into car-buying habits noted a price sensitivity problem for foreign brands – 'Consumers who consider buying a [Chinese] Xiali are three times more likely to get one than those who consider buying a [VW] Polo.'

China's transition means that consumers are changing along with everything else. Expectations of quality and safety are rising, particularly in the wake of the contamination scandals in the past few years. The return of home ownership has boosted the markets for furnishings, kitchens, bathrooms and other home products, WTO accession and the opening up of the market has brought buying a car within reach of many more people. At the same time, the Chinese are reaping the less attractive benefits of a booming economy, working longer hours and finding they have less time for leisure and domestic activities.

Chinese consumers have less time

When I visited B&Q in Shanghai, Mark Ladham, Managing Director Retail, B&Q China, pointed out a pair of customers, one talking to a sales assistant and another taking notes. Ladham has done his research, he knows that a customer will not buy on the first visit and will go to several other stores collecting information before deciding. But Ladham also sees how a changing Chinese society means that people have less and less time for this kind of research, and he knows that strengthening the brand and providing the kind of customer service that builds trust will help keep increasingly time-poor customers returning to B&Q.

B&Q understands that building a brand that works in China must extend from product design right through marketing and distribution to after-sales support, because every element along this path can say something about your relationship with the customer. One of the best-known examples of after-sales service in the brand-customer relationship in China is that established by market-leading appliance manufacturer Haier. Purchasers of Haier appliances know that, should the appliance need repair, Haier technicians will put on shoe covers before they enter the house, use dust covers to protect the furniture, and clear up and vacuum the floor before they leave. This respect for the customer is critical to the relationship.

Another example of building relationships to sell products is that of Yue-Sai Kan Cosmetics, founded in 1992 when make-up was just reappearing in China and was still advertised using pictures of Western-looking blondes. The company's eponymous founder, a Chinese-American TV presenter, personally opened each new sales counter around the country, trained her sales staff and wrote and appeared on the packaging and other promotional materials. She strengthened the relationship with her customers through her TV work and by writing on beauty, both in the Chinese press and in books. With 95 per cent brand recognition, a loyal customer base held by their relationship with Yue-Sai, and sales operations covering 240 cities, the company was an attractive acquisition buy for L'Oreal in 2004.

> We've always believed that brands are as important to the Chinese consumer as they are to anybody, but the way to approach them is different. There are six core equities in a brand – the product itself, the image, the channel, the goodwill, how the brand bonds with the customer and the visuals – the logo, design, etc. In developed markets, branding is mostly about image and the customer. In China, it's much more about the channel and goodwill. Channel because you have got to get the brands to the market and that is something companies struggle with in China, especially reaching third, fourth and fifth-tier markets. Goodwill because you need a licence to operate. The first thing that many companies focus on when they come here is government relations, because they need a licence and they need to understand the regulatory framework.
>
> Scott Kronick, Ogilvy

Localising the brand

> All brands have to reposition themselves. All brands have to take
> their global positioning and twist it into alignment with the
> Chinese view.
>
> Tom Doctoroff , J. Walter Thomson

Brand strategy in China must be long term, not just about short-
term financial gain or market share, and localising is an important
part of that. Just as you will be trying hard to localise by replacing
expats with Chinese staff, you should be trying equally hard to
localise your brand. Interestingly, the top ten issues in the
US-China Business Council's 2007 member survey did not mention
brand-building, although IP protection and competition were
highly ranked. It seems obvious, but surprisingly large numbers of
companies fail to address this issue and assume the brand that sells
abroad will sell just as well in China, to consumers they mistakenly
believe are desperate for foreign products.

A *McKinsey Quarterly* article (Grant, 2000) identified the emerging
Chinese consumer as 'one eager for modern products but with
distinctly Chinese tastes and behaviour'. This is reflected in their
preference for local products, bordering on nationalism. The two
companies with the lion's share of the Chinese computer market,
Lenovo and Founder Technology, are both home-grown, with US
firm Dell a distant third, and domestic brands made up 27 per cent
of car sales in first three quarters of 2007. Food chain KFC has
adapted its format to suit a Chinese customer who prefers to eat in
a restaurant with a group of family or friends, rather than grab a
single meal to take away. Other food brands have developed

> ## Food brands have developed products such as red bean flavour ice cream

products to appeal to the Chinese, such as red bean flavour ice
cream from Unilever, and redesigned packaging to reflect Chinese
colour and design preferences.

It's not just about creating products that match Chinese tastes, companies naturally want to import brands as well. Introducing a brand is time-consuming and expensive, so exploiting brands that are established in other territories is important. Luxury lifestyle company Three on the Bund planned to build its own luxury brand in Shanghai incorporating ten concepts, but without the time and budget to develop all ten from the ground up, the company imported three international brands and introduced the other seven.

And don't forget the most basic element in localising your brand – how your company or product name translates into Chinese. Luckily for Coca-Cola, its name translates as 'you drink, you laugh' (although an urban legend suggests the initial translation came out as 'bite the wax tadpole'), unfortunately for a sportswear manufacturer, its name translated as 'shit'. Names are important to the Chinese, embodying culture and values as well as personality. If you decide to translate the meaning of your product name, rather than just the phonetics, remember that Western names can often be written several ways in Chinese characters, and subtle differences between the meanings can make a big difference to the way your company or product is perceived.

> Your aim is to make a connection between your brand and the customer, and how you do that is very important. Names play a key role. We have done research on Chinese names and what they mean in different parts of the country, to make sure that the name resonates with the customer when it is pronounced in different ways. We do cultural checks and focus groups to make sure the name works. Sometimes the price of entry is really making sure that you get the naming right.
>
> Scott Kronick, Ogilvy

Three on the Bund, an upmarket retailer based in Shanghai, has a portfolio of complementary brands that operate synergistically, but the challenge for many companies is to position localised and imported brands so that they don't cannibalise each other's markets. Knowing what you do now about the size and variety of markets within China, it is easy to see that there are opportunities to run concurrent brands, but it takes careful planning to do this.

Localising a brand may also involve new positioning. Brands that in the West are considered cheap or low-end may occupy a different niche in China. Olay beauty products and Ikea furniture present two examples of this, both being considered downmarket in the US but positioned as prestigious in China. Buick made the mistake of positioning its cars as the type driven by executives, but then producing a cheaper model that failed to live up to expectations.

> Branding is all about creating an emotional as well as a rational bond with the customer. The winning companies don't just take what they have done globally and impose it on the China market. They take the core of what they're trying to communicate globally, and then see how it would work in China. They strike a balance between being local and being international, and they study the Chinese customer and what would resonate with them.

> Scott Kronick, Ogilvy

Extending the brand

> There is a lot of revenue to be made if you extend down and out a little bit.

> Tom Doctoroff, J. Walter Thomson

While luxury brands still aim for the wealthiest Chinese in the biggest cities, the actual size of this market is small and its contribution to worldwide sales for many such brands is only 1–2 per cent. The middle- and lower-income segments of the Chinese population make up 90 per cent of the country's consumer goods market, but few companies have successfully reached these groups, largely because of the risk of diluting or cannibalising their brands. The companies that do market to the broader population have extended their brands vertically and developed cost and pricing strategies that make their products accessible to those on lower incomes. For instance, a vertical branding strategy helped Colgate to capture the largest share of the toothpaste market, through the introduction of formulations at various price points.

An advantage of vertical brand extension is that it avoids some of the costs of launching a new brand, including piggybacking on advertising for the parent brand, but differentiation between brands must nevertheless be clear. Lower-priced brands will obviously be aimed at different market segments, and differentiation may include making changes to the premium brand, such as new packaging, that helps mark the distinctions between them.

> We have a high-end brand and a mid-level brand, linked to different levels of service, specifications, quality and price. We have to make sure that the high-end brand is really high-end, and we have to pay more attention to what we present to the customers, to make sure that the mid-level products don't cannibalise this market. But if you can't avoid it, then it's better to cannibalise yourself than let somebody else do it!
>
> Niels-Erik Olsen, Danfoss

Distribution is an important tool in differentiating between vertical brands

Distribution is an important tool in differentiating between vertical brands, from the type of outlets a product is sold in to making sure that two brands from the same company are displayed on different shelves. Olay, the cosmetic group, sells its cheaper products in supermarkets, but more upmarket ranges, such as the company's Regenerist label, are sold on Olay counters in department stores. This strategy could enhance Olay's chances of keeping its customers as they become wealthier, an important consideration in a market where brand loyalty is in its infancy and incomes are changing rapidly. Motorola and Nokia have also succeeded in capturing market share in different consumer segments without diluting their brand images, selling mobile handsets over an enormous range of prices, from Rmb400 to Rmb9,000.

A vertical brand extension strategy can also work in B2B markets. For example, enzyme company Novozymes offers three brands, high-end, value-added and one for formulators, which encompass not only pricing needs, but also the different quality requirements of different customers.

Brand innovation

> Brand innovation is a way for us to play the game differently.
> I think this is an edge we have over a lot of our Chinese
> competitors. We have two hundred and twenty beer brands
> around the world, so we have a big reservoir of innovation to
> pick from.

> Eric Melloul, InBev

There are advantages and disadvantages to brand innovation,
particularly in China where launching a brand nationally is
extremely challenging and expensive, and regional launches must
all be treated as separate entities rather than simply a geographical
expansion of the same brand. But as Eric Melloul of InBev
commented, in a highly competitive market like beer, innovation
may be the only way to keep ahead of the local competition.

Office supplier Staples and delivery company UPS took a novel
approach when they opened two co-branded shops in Beijing in
October 2007. Known as 'Staples UPS Express', this co-branding
not only shares the risk, but also builds on the separate reputations
of both companies in China, an assumption being that the joint
brand will be greater than the sum of its parts. There are certainly
cost benefits to be gained from launching a brand that has,
essentially, already been launched.

> We are not as big as Siemens or Proctor & Gamble, so we have to
> target the segments where we have leverage, use different
> branding strategies and measure against different parameters. We
> have very good stories to tell. The sustainability and
> environmental angle is good for us, because our products replace
> harsh chemicals and reduce energy consumption. Our social
> record, the standards we apply internally for our employees, is
> another good story. And we have our focus on bio-fuel, which is
> high on the Chinese government's agenda right now. The
> channels we use include relationship-building with key people,
> academia, where we give scholarships and collaborate on joint
> research projects, and PR and branding partners. We don't have a
> big budget for consultants, but we use our money wisely.

> Humphrey Lau, Novozymes

Allocating your branding budget

How you promote your brand in China depends on what you plan to sell, and to whom. Advertising is expensive, and there may be other channels that could be more important for brand-building.

> All the different communications channels and disciplines are thriving at the moment. This is a huge advertising market. Direct marketing is in its infancy but growing very, very fast. Media is interesting because how people get their information is different. Public relations is active, through media channels and event marketing in stores. Choosing between them depends on what you want to communicate and what action you want, for instance FMCG [fast-moving consumer goods] focus their spend on advertising, whereas if you want to influence policies and decision-making, public relations is usually better.
>
> Scott Kronick, Ogilvy

If you don't have a large budget, then focusing on a market is very important. Partnerships, too, can be vital, because branding could be just as much about how you do business as how you promote your products.

> Brand is very important to us in China, for two main reasons. Firstly, we sell business-to-business and we are not the cheapest on the market, so we need a differentiation strategy in our target industry sectors and that depends on brand-building. Secondly, at the corporate level, we need support from the Chinese government if our bio-fuel initiative is going to work, so we need the status that a major brand can bring.
>
> Humphrey Lau, Novozymes

Advertising

The range of opinions about the benefits of advertising in China highlight how critical it is to know your market. Some commentators claim that the Chinese are not as cynical about advertisements as Westerners, but others say that they are more so – 72 per cent of Chinese TV viewers left the room or changed channels when advertisements were shown, according to research carried out by McKinsey in 2004. Both are probably right. To interpret these results and apply them to your business, you would need to know more details about the consumers surveyed, particularly where they live and how much they earn.

Yet despite this air of confusion over the value of advertising, a few numbers tell us that companies see it as essential. Advertising revenues at China's national television network, CCTV, more than doubled between 2000 and 2004, Coca-Cola spent $26.1 million on advertising in China in 2000, the most of any foreign company and twentieth overall, and in 2003 the Chinese advertising market was the third largest in the world at $24 billion. There's no sign of much of a slow-down, CCTV's airtime auction for 2008 brought in 18 per cent more than the sums paid in 2007. Overall, advertising sales are increasing 20 per cent year-on-year compared with a global average of 5 per cent according to China Business Intelligence.

Rocketing costs mean that it is no longer economically feasible for companies to use advertising to build a national brand from scratch. In the early 1990s, Taiwanese noodle company Tingyi spent $60 million on advertising and promotion to build a national brand, and the *China Business Review* (Crocker & Tay) claims that Procter & Gamble spent $1 billion establishing 'Rejoice, Pampers and Safeguard as three of China's best-selling, most-trusted brands, with 50 per cent market share at their peak.' But competition today is far more intense, and it is unlikely that any company could do the same thing again, so most brand launches are regional rather than national. This makes sense when you remember how fragmented the Chinese market is.

Gazumping in TV advertising

Remember the fluidity of contracts, when a signed piece of paper may just be a snapshot of the situation and have little to do with what actually happens? Signing up for an advertising slot does not necessarily mean you will get that slot. Your advertisement may appear at two in the morning when you were expecting to see it at primetime 7pm.

'But I paid my money!' you might say. Unfortunately, another company might have paid more money for the same slot, you've been gazumped.

Advertising costs in China have been driven up by intense competition. Leading international brewer InBev competes with local companies that they describe as 'irrational players'. These companies are willing to spend huge amounts on advertising and promoting their beers to wholesalers and retailers in an attempt to gain volume and market share, at the expense of dramatically depressing profit margins. This attitude can only be adopted by companies that are still supported by soft loans from government and where the profit incentive is low, and such companies continue to exist despite all the changes taking place in China.

> It's expensive, but InBev still focuses a significant proportion of its marketing spend in TV. 'We're a mainstream brand, not a luxury brand. If you want to go after a billion consumers, you have to use TV,' says Eric Melloul, Director of Marketing for InBev. But now the company is not running so many advertisements, rather it is sponsoring shows, and using product placement in popular programmes to gain awareness. Resources are also being shifted to below-the-line activities, especially point-of-sales marketing to 'push' InBev's beers to the consumer.
>
> Melloul also stresses the importance of public relations. InBev sponsors music and sports events, and recently took a group of Chinese journalists to the company's headquarters in Leuven, Belgium. 'The return on investment for that is ten times higher than putting a TV show on air because every one of those guys is going to write a piece on the front page of a newspaper. We also had two primetime documentaries as a result. That has more credibility with consumers than advertisements.'
>
> Eric Melloul, InBev

If you're going to spend a lot on advertising, then yet again I'm going to tell you how important it is to do your research. You cannot afford to direct the kind of sums involved towards the wrong audience or down the wrong media channel, and you may shoot yourself in the foot if you fail to get the messaging right. Brands may need to be local and international at the same time, but messages that work outside China may fail to resonate. Items such as cameras are often marketed in the West on their ease of use, but a Chinese purchaser gains greater face if he or she buys a camera that is packed with the latest technology and is complicated to use.

The cameras may be identical, but the messages are diametrically opposed. There are also numerous lists of 'dos' and 'don'ts' for advertising in China, all stressing the importance of family, groups and the practical benefits of a product, while avoiding bragging, insulting other products and the number four (because it symbolises death).

At the risk of sounding repetitive, don't rush. It can take as long as two or three years to understand the marketplace – where your target audience lies, how to segment different audiences, how best to reach them, which channels to use. China is never a short-term proposition.

Marketing and distribution

Current thinking in China focuses on the experiential side of branding. Yes there's advertising, public relations, direct marketing, but what we call the 'last mile', the experience people have in the stores, is extremely important. So there's a lot of emphasis on sales promotion.

Scott Kronick, Ogilvy

Where and how you sell your products is an important part of your China branding strategy. The tendency of the Chinese to buy a price rather than a brand means that marketing, point-of-sale and other below-the-line activities are essential.

Endorsements and sponsorship can be a successful branding tool in China. Lenovo gained great face in becoming the first Chinese company to be an official 'top' sponsor of an Olympic Games, and the Beijing Olympics has also boosted the currency of sports stars in marketing. However, companies entering into sponsorship deals with sports stars must do thorough checks. Just as you must be aware of the way that local government can apply its own interpretation to national regulations, so too there are strata of sporting authorities, and a sponsorship deal arranged through a local sports association might not be permitted by the relevant national body. Make sure that the person or organisation selling the

> ## Make sure the person selling the rights has the right to sell them

rights owns those rights or has the right to sell them. Your understanding about delivering quality in China will also come into play in sponsorship deals, as details such as uniform colours and the positioning of logos require careful management.

How your products are distributed, displayed and sold will be an integral part of their brand identity. Brand managers must remember that the 'magic' and 'logic' of brand-building are critical. Despite all the research and creativity they may put into devising the perfect display module or the ideal shelf positioning, the distribution network in China is still relatively new and is short on the kind of skills and experience expected elsewhere. Products have been found piled in a jumble in front of an unused display stand and covered in dust. To get the logic, or implementation, right, you will need well-trained and disciplined salespeople who are able to go into shops and make sure that the retailers understand the product and have given it the expected shelf space or displayed it as requested.

Display is important, especially for products where there are a lot of brands on the market, for instance shampoo, where you can find forty brands in a typical hypermarket, instead of the fifteen or so you would expect in the US. Your products may be displayed perfectly one week, but by the next they could have been displaced by a rival product that was able to give the retailer a better deal. And if your customers are fickle and are not going to come looking for your brand, it is clear that a poor shelf position will not help your sales.

Chinese brands

Since privatisation began, we've seen a different type of competitor. They're more professional, pay more attention to costs and focus more on marketing and image than the old state-owned companies.

Enrico Perlo, president, Guala Closures, China

'China needs more brands' was a 2007 headline in the *China Daily*, reflecting the recognition that, despite the fact that so many products sold around the world are made in China, the margins go to the brand owners rather than the manufacturers.

Branded products are still relatively new in modern China. While in the West people are used to brands such as Coca-Cola that are over one hundred years old, China under the state had no need for brands: little choice and even less differentiation meant that consumers simply bought what was available. The new China has changed all that, but the newness of Chinese brands is reflected in the fact that, of the top ten Chinese brands in a 2003 *Forbes* magazine survey, seven were less than twenty-five years old.

Chinese competitors are learning fast. As state-owned companies, they had no need for marketing and sales skills, but the new landscape is pushing them towards a profit-driven model that needs brands to improve the bottom line. There are still companies in China that are willing to sacrifice margins for volume and market share, but there are also Chinese companies developing branding strategies, often with the help of staff they have poached from foreign companies.

Foreign firms may still have the edge when it comes to marketing sophistication, but Chinese firms find it easier to learn about and identify with their domestic customers. As those customers become more savvy about brands, more sophisticated and more individualistic, Chinese companies will be well placed to change with them.

It is also worth noting that Chinese companies are going overseas in increasing numbers, acquiring foreign brands to give them market share and 'instant' brand value. One example was the purchase of IBM's PC division by Lenovo, which was completed in 2005. The deal allowed Lenovo to continue using the IBM brand on Thinkpads and Thinkcentres for five years, and some commentators believed that the Chinese company would not be able to preserve the brand value. But Lenovo has confounded them, feeling confident enough to drop the IBM brand after just three years.

Equally, Chinese companies are using acquisitions to get round the poor image associated with 'made in China'. Appliance company Haier has moved completely away from the 'made in China' label by setting up manufacturing plants overseas, with the largest being in the US. Yes, it's almost the mirror image of foreign companies acquiring Chinese companies, but the reasons are subtly different – while foreign companies buy in China to acquire market share, manufacturing benefits and local knowledge, Chinese companies are looking overseas to buy branding and management expertise.

Chinese companies are also learning the influence of distribution on their brands, choosing retailers that match the brand image they are trying to create. The choice of Bed Bath and Beyond over Wal-Mart in the US says a lot about a company's products for the home. Sponsorship is also starting to play a role, with Haier sponsoring basketball teams in Australia and Saudi Arabia, and also TV and video coverage of US basketball.

Many Chinese companies adopt pricing strategies that reduce the profitability of their brands. Some of the biggest Chinese brands in

Many Chinese companies adopt pricing strategies that reduce profitability

terms of market share, such as Haier and Tsingtao Brewery, are currently not particularly profitable because they are focusing on price wars. The knock-on effect is that there is less money to invest in new products and marketing campaigns. We must assume, though, that these companies find a way to escape this situation – through preferential lending from banks in the party-state family, for example – and therefore competition in China will become even more intense. To survive, foreign companies must do their homework and invest even more in their brands before Chinese companies catch up and overtake.

Meanwhile, the party-state is backing 'the China brand'. Branding of China as a vibrant market economy, and as power on the world stage was the idea behind the celebrations accompanying the holding of the Olympic Games in Beijing in August 2008. What was particularly noticeable at the Games opening ceremony –

described on US TV as 'über-spectacular' (Hibberd, 2008) – was the rich variety of ancient Chinese art and culture on display, both local and national, and the near absence of any reference to China's history of the previous 170 years. The message was clear: modern, post-1978 China is building on the inheritance of China's great past, without so much as a glance at the years of decline. As Wang Yong, secretary-general of the China Brand Association, described it in China Daily online, the image of China – the one it wishes to project to the world – is 'passion, development, harmony and responsibility'. China is its own master, it makes its own image, the message runs. Yet as Joshua Cooper Ramo has argued, the rest of the world holds an 'an unstable cocktail of out-of-date ideas, wild hopes and prejudices.' about the country. It's time business leaders in the West placed their China strategy in a global context.

China takeaways

▌ Know your party-state. Promoting the country as an IT leader is central to its policy of developing China's potential as an internal market.

▌ Know your customer, and understand that customers cannot be considered under a single, 'Chinese' umbrella. You have to research regional differences.

▌ Build your point-of-sale activities, as relationships are extremely important.

▌ Use brand extension carefully, so you don't cannibalise market share where brands overlap.

▌ Use brand innovation to keep ahead of competitors.

▌ Bring all your knowledge to the table when deciding how to allocate your branding and marketing budget.

▌ Be prepared for brand competition to intensify as Chinese companies learn how to capture and develop brand value.

References and bibliography

Chan, R.Y.K. (1999) 'At the Crossroads of Distribution Reform: China's Recent Ban on Direct Selling', *Business Horizons*, September–October.

Crocker, G., and Tay, Y.–C. (2004) 'What it takes to create a successful brand', *China Business Review*, July–August.

Grant, A. (2006) 'The new Chinese consumer', *McKinsey Quarterly*, June.

Hoffe, J., Lane, K., and Miller Nam, V. (2003) 'Branding cars in China', *McKinsey Quarterly*, December.

KPMG (2008) Destination digital: opportunities in China's media and advertising market', www.kpmg.com.

Li, F., Nicholls, J.A.F., Zhou, N., Mandokovic, T., and Zhuang, G. (2003) 'A Pacific Rim debut: Shoppers in China and Chile,' *Asia Pacific Journal of Marketing and Logistics*, vol 15, no 1/2, 115–131.

Choosing China

If you are going to set up business in China, you will have to decide whether to operate as a joint venture or a wholly owned foreign enterprise. But before you can make that decision, you have to ask why you are going into China.

Alan Hepburn, managing director, Three on the Bund, Shanghai

Choosing to go into China must be a business decision, not a country decision, so it's all about asking the right questions, of yourself, of your business and of the wider world. In the preceding chapters, we've looked at all the things you need to learn about China and setting up operations there, from the big picture of China's transformation and the type of organisation that will succeed, to the basic details of how operating in China differs from elsewhere. Now you must work out exactly how China fits into your business strategy, and be clear about the importance of China to your organisation as a whole.

In this chapter, we're going to build a toolkit for analysing the pros and cons of choosing China over another country. We'll look at the political and economic factors that should be taken into account in your analysis, and see how you can explore the sensitivity of your business sector to prevailing and possible future conditions. Using an example, we'll then investigate how to identify which parts of the value chain might sensibly set up in China and the specific managerial challenges each one faces. Once again, we're going to go from the big picture to the details, and hopefully by the end you'll be in the best possible position to make your choice.

B, R, I or C?

Let's assume you're looking at the BRIC countries, Brazil, Russia, India and China. Each of the BRICs has its own attractions, and each has its own hazards. How do you decide between them? Making an evidence-based business decision about very different countries is possible, but complex. You need a systematic process that will allow you to capture as much information as possible, and then enable you to explore how strategies might be affected by the circumstances in each country. Your top team will then have a basis upon which to consider the balance between in-house resources and know-how, and the resources that will be required to take advantage of the opportunities in new territories.

One example of such a method is the globalisation software that I have developed at INSEAD, https://edptools.insead.edu/simulations/globalisation.

There is a simple registration process, involving a password sent to you by return email.

The software helps companies to start learning in an orderly way about the many factors that will affect their decision as to whether or not to enter a new territory. The process involves four steps, which yield one report. At each step, the software provides a 'things to do' list that guides you along the way.

Step one

The first step is to build a country profile, which can be measured against other territories. If you scroll down under China, you will see all the provinces, so you can do the same exercise on a single province, or, if you wish, compare one part in China with another in India. The country (or provincial) profile incorporates economic, business, social and political elements, and builds up a picture of the threats and opportunities that each territory presents. You assess the country in terms of the thirty factors listed. The way you do so is to assign a value to each factor in the range of −10 (worst) to 10 (best).

These factors are broken down into two categories: politics, law and external political relations; and economic structure, policy and external economic relations. They translate into a checklist, the purpose of which is not to enable us to tick boxes, but to help us break down what is always a complicated set of issues as a first step towards reassembling them as inter-related factors that tell us a story about the country. The checklist approach helps us learn, and also to do so on a comparative basis. The political and economic factors are listed in the box below.

POLITICAL AND ECONOMIC FACTORS

Political system

1 Constitutional context: does this help or hinder good governance?

2 Regime: is the regime in transition, or is it consolidated?

3 Government: how does society rate the quality of public goods and services provided by government?

4 Political climate: is leadership united on policy elements?

5 Social structure: how are wealth and resources distributed, as measured by the Gini index?

Legal system

6 Property rights: is the ownership of resources clear and transparent?

7 Patents: are intellectual property rights secure and respected?

8 Corruption: are public officials perceived to be corrupt?

9 Civil strife: is the incidence of strikes, demonstrations, etc., rising or falling?

10 Rebellion/coup d'état/civil war: is there a dissatisfied, organised minority that may become active against the central power?

External political relations

11 Diplomatic position: how much does the country participate in international society?

12 Geographic location: what are the relations with the country's neighbours?

13 Cultural orientation: does the country's culture, whether religious, linguistic, business or constitutional, cross geographical borders?

14 Technology: does the country's technological base depend on foreign supply or is it developing its own?

15 Freedom: are citizens free to travel, translocate, speak?

Economic structure

16 Market size: what is the purchasing power parity (PPP) and potential of the market?

17 Human capital: what is the supply and skill level of labour?

18 Financial system: how effective and efficient is this?

19 Infrastructure: what is the state of energy, water, transport and telecommunications?

20 Natural resources: is the country endowed with natural resources? How important are worldwide fluctuations in commodity prices?

Economic policy

21 Public finances: is the tax system effective and efficient?

22 Monetary conditions: what is the history of inflation and current price performance?

23 Labour markets: how easy is it to hire and fire people?

24 Access to capital: is it easy to raise capital?

25 Local market for corporate assets: can you buy assets readily on an open market?

External economic relations

26 Trade openness: how significant is trade in goods and services in gross national product (GNP)?

27 Inward investment: is the country a significant net recipient of inward direct investment?

28 Ease of doing business: how does the country rank on the World Bank's index for ease of doing business?

29 Exchange rate: is the currency under- or over-valued?

30 Growth: how fast is the national economy growing?

To help you collect and assess relevant data and information about the territory or the territories you are assessing, the software provides a list of websites for you to access information. You can add your own sites. Many of the sites include rankings: for instance, China ranks 94 out of 179 in the 2008 statistical update of the United Nations Development Programme. The UNDP provides definitions of the measures it is taking. The globalisation software provides a calculator to help you convert the data to the scale used for the software. You can check and explore the websites on the software. The box below illustrates the broad areas covered.

Evaluating countries

A number of universities, research organisations and non-governmental organisations publish information on economic and political development. Respected news organisations also contribute with current events and analysis. Building a complete picture of China from this information is time-consuming but essential if you are to base your China decision on more than just a hunch or the latest fad. The websites listed on the software are broken down under the following heading: macro conditions; the transformation of political and business systems; the transformation of societies; competitiveness of industries; and business conditions. Please be aware that the websites are regularly changed.

The scale used in the software for the first step is +10 to -10. China comes out midway, 0, in terms of human development. By comparison, the territories in the OECD – the rich world club of countries, headquartered in Paris – when converted from their rankings in the UNDP human development rankings, range from +5 (Mexico) to +10 (Switzerland or Norway). At the other end of the scale, Sierra Leone, which ranks at 179 on the UNDP human development index, scores -10 on the globalisation software.

When you have built your country profile, the software sums the values you assigned to the thirty factors. These factors are divided into two categories, 'politics' and 'economics'; 'politics' is measured on the vertical and 'economics' is measured on the horizontal plane. The pair of 'politics' and 'economics' intersect at one point. If you are comparing a number of territories, you can compare their positions on the matrix. What is the implication, for instance, of country X being evaluated more negatively in 'politics' and less so on 'economics'? Should we go back and ask why we have assigned the values that we have? This software, in other words, is *not* designed to provide an answer as to whether we should or should not enter such and such a territory. It is designed as a structured learning tool to help us learn about the territories we are examining.

The second step is to convert the country profile into an industry-sensitivity profile, thereby isolating the opportunities and challenges of the country-industry profile. This second step is asking us the question: how sensitive is your industry sector to each one of thirty factors in the country profile? This is important because it begins to separate out the country risk factor from the industry risk factor.

The third step adds information about the sensitivity of the industry you are in to the political and economic conditions of the country you are wishing to enter in order to assess the impact of opportunities and challenges on the different parts of the value chain. Here we are separating out the parts of the value chain in the industry sector in the country or countries.

The final step is to anticipate the managerial implications for setting up the project – whether the project is no more than setting up an office, entering a joint venture or developing a marketing organisation. This project, whatever it turns out to be, may be compared with other projects in the other BRIC countries. By making the comparison in as thorough a way as possible, you will be on the way to learning about the costs and the benefits to your business of going into China. Equally, the process might reveal that going into China is too risky or expensive.

An example

The best way of explaining the software to yourself is to start playing with it. The example here is from a presentation I made to a mining company in 2006. Figure 9.1 shows two profiles: one of China in 2006 (China 2006) where I used the indices available on the internet.

The other profile is my discounting as many factors as possible to create the scenario for a China crash (China Crash) – the nightmare scenario for the China leadership. Note that I was working on a different scale to the one now presented on the internet.

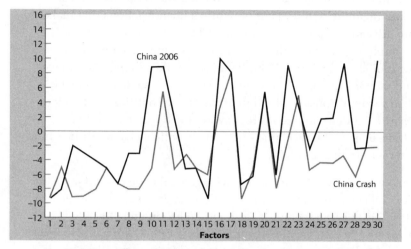

FIGURE 9.1 STEP 1: China 2006 and China crash assessment based on politics and markets factors

Since each of the indices uses its own metrics, I convert them to a range of -10 to +10, using the calculator on the software. The resulting profile in Figure 9.1 represents the conventional wisdom regarding China in 2006. Although the political and legal systems (factors 1–9 on the x-axis) are not valued positively, the consensus is that Tibetan and Turkic demands for autonomy in western China do not pose much of a threat to the regime (factor 10). This may seem surprising, given the attention to Tibet in Western media, and the tensions in the province. But that has to be weighed against the determination of Beijing to defend the unity of the country, as well as the geopolitical advantage of strengthening China's position in the Himalayas. China's diplomatic relationships have improved rapidly with entry to the WTO, membership in Asian regional forums (11), and a solid record as a responsible participant in UN agencies. But China's geographic location (12), with its long sea and land frontiers, still throws up difficulties, such as disputes over islands with Japan or the Philippines that have to be resolved.

Not least, public opinion in south-east Asia, Japan, Russia and India, worries about whether China, once wealthy and powerful, will behave aggressively or consolidate a reputation for being a responsible global citizen. China scores relatively low in terms of cultural orientation (13), a reflection of a sharp rise in Chinese chauvinism, which finds its way into a host of actions that make life difficult for foreign businesses. China also scores low on technology (14), reflecting a continued dependence on foreign technologies, despite accomplishments in developing its science and technology base. The very low score on freedom (15) records the Freedom House evaluation of the lack of political and civic liberties. It does not record the favourable opinions that the Chinese have of how China's open door policies have resulted in a freer and richer country.

Not surprisingly, the profile shows a general consensus that China does better on economics than on politics. In terms of market size (16), China is the second-largest national economy after the US measured in purchasing power parities (PPP). There has also been a notable improvement in human capital (17), as the disasters of the Cultural Revolution fade into the past, when a generation missed schooling. The financial system (18), still under the party's thumb, is effective in being able to concentrate massive resources on the projects that its members choose to invest in, but the efficiency of capital use in China is half that of India, hence the low score.

On infrastructure (19), China scores low overall because there is still a long way to go before the government achieves its 2020 goal of completing a road system comparable with that developed in the US in the 1950s. But if you wanted to refine your research by using this same method to profile say three or four provinces, you would see huge variations. For example, the infrastructure in the Pudong business zone in Shanghai, or in the growth hubs along the coastline around the Yangtse Delta, the Pearl River Delta and the Bohai Sea region, are comparable with those in developed countries. Heavy government investment in developing the infrastructure of central, northern, western and south-western China will yield impressive results by 2020, but for the moment, the availability of rail, road, ports, airports as well as telecommunications is not uniform across the country.

China scores quite high on natural resources (20), given the abundant river waters flowing from the western highlands eastwards to the coastal regions; the availability of coal reserves, and the fact that up to 40 per cent of the country has still not been fully explored for minerals. In addition, China is not self-sufficient in food. But the availability of these resources is not enough to meet China's demand for imported feedstuffs, minerals and fuels. Most importantly, the relative availability of natural resources is offset by the heavy pollution caused by the regime's insistence on keeping growth rates as high as possible. China is probably the most polluted country in the world, with severe fallout in terms of human health and environmental damage.

The profile also shows considerable variations in economic policy performance. The consensus view for 2006 was that China's public finances (21) were not transparent. The government has rightly been phasing out tax concessions for foreign businesses, and opening capital markets to foreign participation through joint ventures with local institutions. But these, and other, improvements in the functioning of the tax and financial systems have not altered the fact that the two remain joined at the hip of the communist party. In 2006, monetary policy (22) was judged very favourably, although there were strong inflationary signs building up in the form of property and financial market bubbles. These inflationary pressures are closely related to the negative view of the regime's perceived under-valuation of the currency (29), and the very rapid growth of the money supply resulting from the abundant supply of US dollars into the system. Access to capital (24) for companies is judged as marginally negative, there was a gradual opening up of competition in the provision of credit. But the firm hand of the party on the flow of funds ensures plenty of opportunities for companies in the communist family to benefit from privileged access, not available to private Chinese firms or to foreign multinationals. Finally, the regime has allowed a market for corporate assets to develop, as part of its longer-term approach to developing a highly competitive 'socialist' market economy –

socialist here referring to the continued hegemony of the party across both the political and economic system.

For external economic relations, China scores very highly on inward direct investment (27) and economic growth (30). Foreign investors from around the world have flooded into China to exploit the low labour costs and to set up shop in a fast-growing market. Up to 60 per cent of the value of Chinese exports is accounted for by foreign-owned companies that have set up production platforms there. Growth rates have lifted from an official 8 per cent a year in the early 2000s, to over 10 per cent per annum since 2005–2006. There are two main reasons for this rise in growth: one is the abundance of financial resources in a fast-growing economy, where 45 per cent of national income is saved. Chinese companies have restructured, and are rich in retained earnings; households save against rainy days in a country where there is next to no public welfare provision.

China scores just positive on trade openness (26), despite the fact that hardly any emerging market is as open to imports as China – now one of the world's top importers, with imports growing faster than exports. The reason for this consensus view may be that China runs huge current account surpluses – the inevitable counterpart to the high level of savings. As long as the reasons for these high savings remain, then China may be considered as running a structural surplus. This is one of the prime weaknesses in the global trading system: China's top export market is the European Union, followed closely by the US. The EU cannot close its markets easily because most of its twenty-seven member states are small economies, wide open and dependent on the world economy. Only the US is capable of closing its markets abruptly. The conclusion to take away for foreign business people operating in China is that China is not a closed economy; rather it is an over-exposed economy. Its future is interdependent as never before with the rest of the world.

Table 9.1 China has a long way to go: implications for business

	Ease of doing business	Starting business	Deal with licences	Employ workers	Register property	Get credit	Protector investor	Pay taxes	Trade across frontiers	Enforce contract	Close business
Singapore	1	9	5	1	13	7	2	2	1	4	2
US	3	4	24	1	10	7	5	76	15	8	18
Hong Kong	4	13	60	23	58	2	3	3	3	1	1
Taiwan	50	103	128	148	24	48	64	91	29	92	13
China	83	135	175	86	29	84	83	168	42	20	57
Russia	106	50	177	101	45	84	83	130	155	19	80
India	120	111	134	85	112	36	33	165	79	177	137

Source: IFC, The Doing Business in Project, 2008 rankings

Choosing China

Ease of doing business (28) has been left to last. This is a very valuable index for international business people seeking to get a handle on the risks and opportunities of doing business around the world. The International Finance Corporation asks people ten questions about their experiences of doing business in one hundred and eighty-one territories (Table 9.1). China comes in at number 83. There are several points to take from China's ranking in this index.

First, Singapore and Hong Kong rank first and fourth. Singapore, in some ways a model for China's communist leadership, is a small, one-party, city state and is run by well-educated cadres. Hong Kong, which returned to Chinese sovereignty in 1997, is China's prime financial market, and stands as a benchmark for mainland China.

Second, the US rates third in terms of ease of doing business, a measure of how much more complex it is to do business in China. There is still a long way to go before the regulatory environment for business in China meets world standards. Third, China ranks ahead of both Russia and India, while Brazil is even further behind at number 125. That places China as the best-of-class among the BRICS.

However, fourth, a glance along the ten questions into which the poll is broken down gives an idea of the managerial resources that have to be devoted to starting a business, dealing with licences, hiring and firing employees, getting access to credit, protecting investors from theft, paying taxes, managing imports and exports and closing a business. Only in registering property and in contract enforcement is China ranked by business people as high on an international scale.

This country profile for China 2006 is then reduced to one number, which enables you to compare your judgement of the territory against others. In this case, I assess China 2006 against a worst-case scenario of a crash in that year (Figure 9.2). The software totals the fifteen political and fifteen economic factors, and converts them to yield one number on a matrix, composed of a vertical scale of +10 to -10 for politics, and economics on the horizontal. Remember that China 2006 summarises a consensus view, drawn from internet indices of China as a place to do business as of 2006; and China crash is a scenario where I discount as many factors as possible to give an idea of what a worst case would look like. Most China watchers consider that a crash would involve a divided leadership facing an angry and organised population, and economic growth that has slowed down or been brought to a halt.

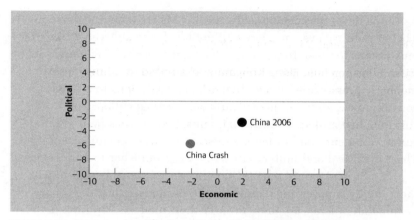

FIGURE 9.2 STEP 1: simplified matrix for China 2006 and China crash assessment

As Figure 9.2 shows, China 2006 is ranked negatively in terms of politics and positively in terms of economic performance. If the same analysis had been done in 1990, one year after the regime crushed the student demonstrations on Tiananmen Square in June 1989, China 1990 would occupy a place on the matrix similar to that of a hypothetical China crash in 2006. In 1990, growth was down, the country was isolated internationally, the international communist system was disintegrating, and Western capitalism under US leadership was emerging triumphant from the Cold War struggle. Comparison between 2006 and 1990 gives a measure of what has been accomplished, but also of how far China has to go before it becomes a developed country. Conversely, if we revert to considering the lower point on the matrix as representing a China crash now, we may draw the conclusion that even under the worst conditions, China's achievements to date would still leave the country way above many other emerging markets. The achievements in reconstituting human capital, in building infrastructure, and in creating an increasingly sophisticated corporate sector and market economy are not so easily dismantled.

Put another way, it is conceivable that continued pragmatic management of China's transformation from a closed, state-run system towards an open market economy may well lead to a de facto change of regime.

As China develops economically, its citizens are bound to demand a better political system. They will not like being cultivated like mushrooms for ever, living in the dark and covered by manure. Indeed, foreign businesspeople are well advised to follow closely the many press stories about citizens' angry reactions to official corruption expressed in poorly built schools that collapse on children, bad milk distributed to infants, toxic wastes poured into scarce water supplies, or land confiscation without compensation. These are bread-and-butter battles that the regime has to win if it is to guide China forward over the coming decades. And it has to win them not by suppressing dissent, but by demonstrating to ordinary people that officials are there to serve their interests. Opinion polls show that there is still a lot of work for the regime to do in dispelling the cynical view among the public about what drives officialdom.

Before moving to the second step of the process, it's worth reminding ourselves that what we have done here is to make an assessment of China as one country, when we know that it is made up of twenty-three provinces, five autonomous regions, and four privileged municipalities. Income gaps vary widely, and have widened since China's opening to the world. So, to refine our search for the best location to invest in China, we can use the same procedure as we have just gone through, and compare several places.

Step two

All the political and economic factors that make up the country profile will feed into the second step of the process, which is to determine how sensitive your business sector is to the criteria used to assess the territory. Some of these criteria will be of general concern, such as the efficiency of the tax system or the quality of education provided. Others may be local, such as the threat of civil disobedience or civil war, or the quality of transport. Because all will affect your business to some degree, the country profile has to be related to the needs of your company. This is what we begin to do now.

Here, we use the same criteria as in the first step, but this time the factors are multiplied according to how important they are to your sector, with those that have no effect being multiplied by 0, and those that are critical being multiplied by 10. The resulting graph will reveal the cut-off points for threats (troughs) and opportunities (peaks), as illustrated in Figure 9.3 from the China 2006 profile. The software enables you to chose the level at which you wish to make the cut-off points. The idea is to isolate a sufficient number of variables that are useful to start interpreting into data for managerial use. In this case, the cut-off points are drawn at 35 either side of par – sufficient to be able to isolate peaks and troughs.

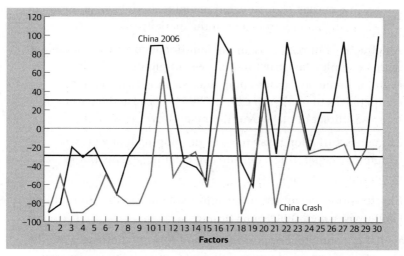

FIGURE 9.3 STEP 2: analysis of industry sensitives for China 2006 and China crash assessment

Here is the list of opportunities for your business sector, identified by the software for China 2006; it will be familiar to those operating in China:

▌ The regime faces no serious opposition at home, though there are plenty of local challenges that officials face every day.

▌ Its international standing is high and it is wide open to trade and foreign investment.

▌ There is significant investment in developing human capital.

▌ For mining companies, China has considerable natural resources.

▌ Monetary conditions are pro-growth, though inflation remains a concern, and the economy is growing fast as its potential unfolds.

In terms of challenges:

▌ It is as well to remember that China is ruled by a communist party, which controls political and market levers that are not usually available to Western governments.

▌ Party officials at all levels enjoy extensive influence over the courts.

▌ The leadership has acknowledged property rights as key to a flourishing market economy, but patents – both local and foreign – are not adequately protected in the marketplace.

▌ An effective but relatively inefficient financial system, combined with a complex tax structure, throws up plenty of challenges – even for financial service companies seeking to bring their competences to market in China. This is because the party exercises direct tutelage over financial flows, as we have seen.

▌ China has still a long way to go in developing home-grown technology capabilities, despite eye-catching events in the development of satellites.

▌ Shortcomings in infrastructure add to the difficulties of building China-wide operations.

This list of contextual opportunities and threats/challenges are the stuff out of which you have to anticipate some of the managerial conundrums of your proposed China operation.

Step three

The next step is to feed this list of contextual opportunities and challenges for your business sector into an analysis of what your company wants to do, if managers decide to go into China. Obviously, this decision is shaped by the knowledge that your top management team have about your corporate resources, and by the view that they come to hold about how the market in China is likely to grow in the coming decades. The decision will also probably be influenced by what and where shareholders consider their company should be investing, and by other locations for business development that attract your top team.

Whatever the motivations driving the organisation, there can be no doubt that investing in a country as complex as China requires a prolonged learning process. We may want to go in deep, but if we have limited in-house knowledge of the country, we would be well advised to learn from Deng Xiaoping. One of Deng's favourite maxims was to 'cross the river by feeling the stones'. In other words, give your organisation time to accumulate shared knowledge about operating in China. So the third step is to get an idea of how parts of the value chain are affected by prevailing conditions, as a prelude to thinking through which part or parts of the value chain you may wish to consider developing there.

Figure 9.4 represents the effect of the opportunities and challenges facing mineral providers on entering the China market. The vertical axis totals the values of opportunities and challenges, and the horizontal axis lists components of a generic value chain. Since the chain in effect represents a complex flow of authoritative transactions within a company, it is best understood as illustrating a permanent feedback process, such that inbound logistics at the end of the scale feeds into operations and procurement. The software is designed to answer the question: which part of the value chain is most favourably influenced by the balance of opportunities and challenges? We may note that this is not the same as asking: which part of the value chain should we get into? My judgement, for instance, on the impact of the balance of opportunities and challenges on operations and procurement for minerals suppliers to the China market is relatively favourable. The party-state wants to keep growth high and the steel industry is hungry for iron ore and other minerals. Client relations and services appear a relative problem area, so if the company goes in, it will have to acquire the capabilities to make up for what the top team identifies as in-house deficiencies.

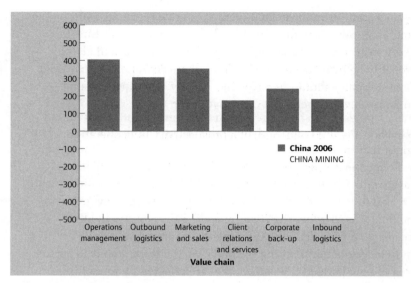

FIGURE 9.4 STEP 3: effects on the corporate value chain for a mining group (China 2006)

Inbound as well as outbound logistics are identified as problem areas in this presentation, but here the solution is largely in the hands of the government, and the execution of its ambitious transport infrastructure programme. To the extent that bottlenecks are created, as demand for iron ore outpaces the ability of miners to supply the market, there is an evident impact for the company in terms of pricing policy. Overall, it has to think through how to capture as much value as it can in each segment of the value chain, while building on its reputation to the host country as a reliable supplier, and to home country public opinion as a company with high ethical standards. This raises important questions about what it can do in China as part of its global corporate policy, and what it cannot or should not do. What it can do, for instance, is to insist on high quality of services and on safety standards. But what it cannot do is to take for granted the local protection of patents, or that it can place as much reliance on written contracts as in other territories. As a mining company, it would be well advised to tread carefully if it is thinking of starting mining operations in China: the country has the highest mining accident rate in the world, and the party-state is undecided about whether to attract inward investors or to keep mining resources under party-state control.

Step four

Let us assume here that your top team decides to explore entering the China market through one or more parts of the value chain. The task here is to assess the managerial challenges of setting up the operation in light of the balance between in-house resources and the image that has been built up in your top team's mind about the opportunities and challenges of a prospective China operation.

In Figure 9.5, the China 2006 country-industry-value chain assessment yields a varied and complex picture of the managerial challenges involved in setting up one or more parts of the value chain. Given demand in the market for the product, the entry, operations and sales functions should not prove too problematic. But human relations policies will need to be crafted to local conditions, and that will certainly entail investment in training. And, in this assessment, thought will have to be given to dealing with what appears to be a problem in logistics.

Overall, the assessment for the value chain sub-section project in the example for China 2006 is positive. So now is the time to put some numbers on the project, where you estimate the anticipated cost of the project relative to the anticipated benefits. A crucial component of both costs and benefits will be the learning process. On the cost side, you will need to anticipate the cost of the unavoidable trial-and-error process that awaits you, and on the benefit side, you will need to evaluate the potential of opportunities that will open up. We are back where we began at the first step in the process, where in effect we are learning about China's potential relative to other territories.

In Figure 9.5, I have also illustrated how much more problematic it would be to operate one or more parts of the value chain in a China crash scenario. The obvious point to note is that the economics of poorly defined projects would immediately become visible and the managerial problems across all functions would be much greater. So, what is the probability of such a China crash? Judged on a four-point scale, say of low, medium, high and imminent, we are on safe ground to say for the moment that the probability is somewhere between low and medium – in other words, not to be discounted.

There is plenty of tinder lying around in China to spark a conflagration. The Chinese leadership is only too aware of the challenge, and you would be advised to factor this awareness into your estimate of the country's long-term evolution. The lesson the leadership took from the events building up to the 1989 Tiananmen Square crackdown against the student demonstrations is that under no circumstances must the leadership become divided. As Deng Xiaoping stated: 'The CCP status as the ruling party must never be challenged. China cannot adopt a multi-party system.'

Two conclusions flow from this comparison of operating two prospective projects in a China 2006 assessment and in a China crash scenario. The first is that because not all parts of the prospective value chain will show high returns, lower return projects may be anticipated as viable under China 2006, but not under the China crash scenario. Second, that rigorous assessment in choosing the right projects in the value chain is essential. Given that the crash scenario cannot be discounted, the project in a China 2006 assessment would have to yield above-average returns to account for the risk.

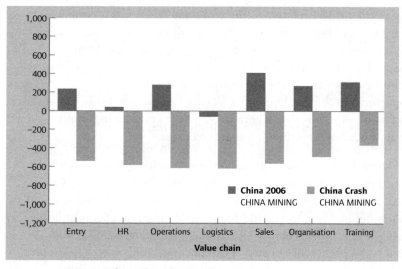

FIGURE 9.5 STEP 4: the value chain sub-section

Business not country

The method of assessing country-industrial and value chain-project risk described above ensures that we evaluate relative projects in different territories, and not the territories themselves. In other words, we do not go to China because every other firm in our industry is there. We go there because we estimate that the return on our anticipated project in China is going to turn out better than, say, our estimated project in Russia, India or Brazil. What we have done is to internalise the opportunities and challenges that our top team considers inherent to operating in China, and incorporated those opportunities and risks into our project. The China risk is embedded in the project.

This approach, hopefully, has helped us to start organising our learning about China. The whole point about learning is that you begin with a vague and woolly idea that it may be a good thing to invest in the one of the BRICS, and that as you proceed, these vague and woolly thoughts coalesce into a hypothesis. As your top team continues to learn, you alter the hypothesis in the light of evidence, and so on until your hypothesis takes shape in the form of a project that you can attach numbers to. My advice is that the *last* thing you do is attach numbers to a project. It is comforting to jump straight for the numbers, but all you will be doing is attaching numbers to a woolly idea, or a half-baked hypothesis. Wait until you have worked through as many of the managerial issues as you reasonably may be expected to anticipate and then put numbers to the project. That's scientific management in action. John Maynard Keynes came up with a nice definition (in other circumstances) of the scientific approach: 'When the facts change, I change my mind. What, sir, do you do?'

China takeaway

▌ Going into China is a business decision, not a question of following the herd. You must use the appropriate analytical tools to help you make the best decision for your business.

▌ Don't try to take any short cuts, money and time invested now will pay off in the long run.

▌ Remember that the key factors in China are relationships and time. The world's oldest civilisation may be moving fast, but it has patience and so must you.

Last word

There are common themes in what people operating in China have told me: things change quickly; competition is intense; implementing the rule of law is still in its infancy; research is crucial; and trying to understand China is key. There are also differences: some companies work best through joint ventures while others operate more effectively on their own; some companies barely cover their costs in China while others make a noticeable contribution to global earnings; and some guard their intellectual property fiercely while others don't give a damn.

Sometimes China behaves like a market economy and sometimes it doesn't. China is on its own trajectory, neither converging with the Western model nor diverging into independence. China must do business with the world, and the world must do business with China. What you make of it will ultimately be up to you and how your organisation executes its China strategy.

Things in China happen fast, and that means that you have to learn fast. The best way to do so is to get stuck in. Good luck.

Index